EATING SITTING DOWN

Selected Poems by
Shawn Michael Morris

Order this book online at www.trafford.com
or email orders@trafford.com

Most Trafford titles are also available at major online book retailers.

Printed in Victoria, BC, Canada.

ISBN: 978-1-4269-1866-7 (sc)
ISBN: 978-1-4269-1865-0 (dj)

Library of Congress Control Number: 2009937970

*Our mission is to efficiently provide the world's finest, most comprehensive book publishing
service, enabling every author to experience success. To find out how to publish your book,
your way, and have it available worldwide, visit us online at www.trafford.com*

Trafford rev. 2/5/2010

 www.trafford.com

North America & international
toll-free: 1 888 232 4444 (USA & Canada)
phone: 250 383 6864 ♦ fax: 812 355 4082

Happiness is when what you think,
what you say, and what you do are in harmony.
~ Mahatma Gandhi ~

This book is dedicated to family and friends past present
and future, who have touched my life in un-measurable ways.
Thank you

CONTENTS

FOR SAUL

What will be, will be and is
We can't live in dreams or illusions
Optimism and pessimism are apart of the journey
But all there is, is now
Accept and grow and move forward
Acknowledge anger, humility, anguish and rejection
Embark on a spiritual adventure
Allow yourself transformation
Give yourself the permission to fail
And the gift to learn from it
Live passionately, discerning to explore all
The radiant chasms that make up our personalities
Incredible potential lies within each remarkable individual
Do you respect people as they are?
Can we not achieve a common peace?
We must look within ourselves
To find our own security
Don't rely on extrinsic sources
That give us temporary praise and self worth
Why is their so much learned naiveté?
We must be freed of our compulsions
Experience love deeply
Have true compassion
And achieve a united humanity
Everyone's on a mission
But is it there lives that are being lived
Are you destined for maturity
We live in a competitive world
One filled with prejudice and fear
Our needs are simple;

LOVE and RESPECT

~ WE JUST WANT TO FEEL PRECIOUS ~

This indeed my friend you helped everyone to recognize

1

UNIVERSAL FORUM

The things that do merge
With a surge of creativity
Preserving the essence of flow
Do know and go together.
Paralleled and converged
Surging ahead
Never diverging
Creating love in being
Peeling away to the core
Of seeing what's freeing
Sometimes inducing a state
That is more complete
Perchance by fate
~ I will leave you this to contemplate:
.........Are you in the zone
            When the universe plays you?

INQUISITION

Is your immediate ego
Heading in every direction
Is the dissection of thought
What ought to be forgotten
While letting your busy mind go
What is the selection of pertinence
That's sometimes beyond grasp
Of a soulful perfection
What's your absolute task
Might I ask?
        ....Just a question

REPMUTATION

A reputation will be yours to keep
It can be distorted and changed
Rewarded and reaped
Alteration potential, will always be there
And others may claim it
Without any cares
Even being outright
The owner in full,
With no effort at all
You may feel the pull
You see peoples attention
Paid to much to the masses
Can be a costly mistake
While your life suddenly passes
When you are trying so hard
To be another person,
Who will you decide to discard
Because there is nothing worse than
Being someone who your not,
Or creating any unions
Just because you thought
That another individual
Would help your rep improve
If you don't know who you are
Admit it, what's to lose
By learning as you go
As you grow
It takes some time
To get to know
Yourself in this world
Of rep-mutations

LIFE FORMS

The inspiration
From many realizations
Of how truly blessed
And precious is,
        My life;
            has form

Personal manifestation
Mental congregation
So much elation
That I get to yet to feel;
        Beyond many born

Many aspirations
Beyond any calculations
Allow instinctive purity
And powerful positivity;
        This should be the norm

Pure born motivation
Lends to any equation
The power within
We can choose;
        Not to be torn
           ~my life has form~

TUNING FORK

Imagine
If you could catch
The words of bad news
While aloft in the air
Would you re arrange any
Before the hit your ear
Would there still be allure
To endure the making of time

COLUMBINE

A seething violence stirs
Undetected by most
The convincer is convinced
Everything is fine
IS IT, ARE WE?
Is prevention unpreventable
Tell me who decides
And how long does it take
When you know it's too late
Has ignorance prevailed
Again
Can't we refrain
To avoid such pain?
Avoid trying
To figure the unfigurable
Because sometimes the unfigurable just is
Don't accept it,
Acknowledge it
Move on
Be strong
Rid yourself of your wrongs
And just get along
Thank, love, live and give
You are your own rainbow
Glowing, radiant, colorful and vibrant
Create your own fairytale
Sooth the seething
Challenge what stirs you

ALL IN TIME

Timelessness
The purest
Of all space
Deeper than any ocean
A million cosmos it does embrace
No momentum
No limit
Just everything happening
Always in it
To be enjoyed
And taken in
It's now, I recon
That things again begin
It is impossible
Too not pass by
But getting to caught up
With the how and why
Of the everyday routine
Can make everything
Certainly seem
Like a cluster fuck
Of madness
And while most sapients
Are saddened....
While snowballing
Out of control...
I remember
When we all had less
And yet everything
Seemed so much,
More whole
What time was it then
I wonder in this blunder
We're late again,
All in time I guess

VOIDING THOUGHT

When not thinking
Are you shrinking
Any possibility of distraction,
Including the reaction
Of even letting go?
Accept the satisfaction
Of not having to know
What will become
Immediately…
Is wanting to know
That at the sum
Of it all
It all adds up,
Unreasonable?
Once seasoned
It may become easier
To beckon the call
Of stillness

Some self proclaimed astute
Have considerably less acute
Insight… despite whether I'm right,
What more needs to be added?

EXSESSIVE PROGRESSIVE

We're sinking
Into the whole
Of dysfunction,
What a critical
Somehow political
Un functioning
Punctuated junction
That our inhumane
Most often insane
Humanity is about facing
It's imperative we act
Instead of chasing
Fallacies for show
Staring at this fact blindly
You know will not help change
Or re-arrange evolution
The minor detail
In any solution
Is progressive action
We must set sail
In this frail time
Perhaps having a say
In if the stars are to align
It's not hard to define
"All aboard"
Is it?

AWARNESS

What are we
Without awareness
Who are we
Before awareness takes form
Before we are born
We are blessed with our life
Why is conceivability's horn
Blown so loud
That we are deafened
By inconceivability's
Except for this....
And that... it's all real
But then exactly what's reality
Now that may depend
On how you feel
Are you aware of this?

ONWARDS

A roundabout journey
Interlaced
And in your face
What is now.....
Predictable and adaptable
Is a pace
That co-insides
With my art
Of misdirection
Oh that whiplash sensation
Can cripple

BLENDER

Is it possible to lend a hand to experience
Rather than having your experience/es
Lend a hand to you?
I think it's necessary
To add to experience
And let experience add too
To what you do,
Visa Versa, on we go
Never ceasing to do exactly this
Become your experiences
And let them become you
From the essence within and beyond
You happen
Blending simultaneously
Becoming all
     Becoming one
          Becoming more
               Becoming none,
A congregation of elemental forces
Creating a supplementation
Of subjective matter
That may or may not matter

THIS IS A RECORDING

What's Blasé
Becomes passé
So very fast
In this day
Our new foray
Seems to be
To learn to forget
I regret to inform you......
Call 911
It's an emergency

MIND THE SIGNS

My mind is hung with an open sing
Flashing with cosmic blues
Everybody's charging in
For a piece of the pie
Is there a need to ask why…
Why sometimes is it so hard
To say goodbye

Is my open mind a closed sign
The exploding cosmos blew
Why is there a price for love
Do you even like pie
Why not ask the needy
Sometimes goodbye is ok
As long as you are open for business

CROPPED CIRCLES

If you can emulate the people who are living in a way
That show integrity, balance and respect
Surround yourself if you can, by these individuals
It's a given their inspiration does tend to infect

CAUSEWAY

Eyes to the sky
The blue refraction makes you high
Shine with the sun
Unite, become one
Let your feet form to the ground
Take the time to look around
Appreciate the butterflies
Feel the freshness and rebirth
After a summers rain
Accept and exist
Freely and in tune
Create an embrace
Search out for the sound of a loon
Tranquil and harmonious
Compassionately passionate
With yourself at least for sure
Realize contentment
It's meant to be

UNTITLED

We have purpose because we feel
That's what makes inconcievabilities real

CHEMTRAILS

When the moon goes down
Do the birds still fly
Can you hear the trees
                in our falling forests
That can't be seen with the eye

Like a jet flying oh so fast
That's only now what we know
Soon something will go faster
Then the jet becomes so slow

Is this called evolution?
Some call it the unknown
It's an enigma of curiosity
For which the answers
                we'll always roam

RESIDULES

Most people bear a burdening weight
That resides in the back of their minds,
The world can and will be a miserable place
When you think you're owed something in time

ENHANCEMENT STANCE

Nothing needs to get bigger
From implanting I figure
Addressing what's destructing
The natural state
Seems to be busting
Can you relate
To such a fucked thing
We did it, admit it
Do you suddenly hear
The ticking, it's sticking
The clock is not tricking
The hand that's been dealt,
Nor my spirit or my health.
Is the onus on my self
To enhance all quality
No time to stall I see
As I'm deafened
By the clock

EMBEDDED INSIDE OF ME

Internally I find
We need to unwind

CRUTCHES

The past it'll last
If you dwell too much,
Adjust accordingly,
Move foreword,
Make an effort not to clutch

BACK EDDY

We struggle by nature
Against the nature of reality,
Hoping to avoid certain change
We must clearly see that fate is pure
Understanding the constant re-arrange
As the ultimate Truth
Weather pain and/or pleasure
We must selflessly go with the flow
Some of life will sooth
But holding to tight onto this treasure
We set ourselves up for certain suffering
As we go,
As we're going,
As we're gone

MR. JONES

Everything by nature is chaos complete
Yet it all seems to fit into place
Is there any way a baby chooses it's time
When it finds a birth into this crazy race

Keeping up with the Jones's we are made to believe
Will keep us content all along our ways
But in this process of getting ahead
We fall behind, a shortcoming per say

The future is a rational based on mere theory
A concept that quickly becomes worn and frayed
Retarding our ability to be purely captivated
By each of the individual happenings every day

SYNERGY

Confessing to obsessing
With the things that keep you guessing
Blanketed in mystery
With the uncertainties of what is, feeling free
Dispersing ever randomly
The moments that we clearly see
Our surroundings with synchronicity
Allowing a connection with a beautiful simplicity
Whether a glassy wave or a snow covered peak
Or just the feeling of a faint summers breeze on you cheek
Perhaps a slight heightening of awareness it could be
We're all equal in fairness I see
Is there ever a time when we're in pure control
Or simply guided by a faith from the depths of the soul
Whatever the answer, to become a part of this rhythm
We must seek out to unleash this sought after synergism
For only then, will we be fully tuned in
And during these certain moments, you'll feel timelessness begin

POP FLIES

Do you have to really live
In order to be alive?
What do you strive for
Make decisions that give
One: longevity
Too, maturity
Three strikes your out
No need for any more
Foul balls to the wall

SLOW TRICKLE

By all means it's intangible
Yet without question the whole of our parts
Some theories happen to put it
As the place where everything starts

It's the softest of all substance
And can't really be grasped
Its effect is fluid evolution
So with time as it's passed

We're limiting her quality
Creating a certain dismay
Soon all that is will be damned
Powerless to our absurd modern day

We must rapidly unite
Yet has our trickle of a pace
Passed the point of no return
We'll wave goodbye in such disgrace
Water…. you made of?

.......would it not make sense
To take the agonizing self
Out of self agonizing

17

WHAT THE FUSS

It tends to be
And this just is
A tendency
In this business
We call life
Is it really
That much harder
To simply simplify
I wonder why
By our own accord
We're floored by implementation
Of basic equations
In our adverse, perverse
Fabricated nature
We complicate
What is complicating
Which is primarily us
Right off the cuff
To begin with
We must begin this
Abridge, Instate, Commence
We're late in our survival
Jump off the fence
Our revival is now

QUICKER PICKER UPPER

It seems not a pure love
Perhaps cowardly in fact
For most immediate pleasures
We must learn how to act
With enough personal respect
Looking beyond what things seem
We get true understanding
Not passing life in a dream
Although certain things without question
Do captivate some beyond
What fits now in time and space
Is always soon to be gone
Relative to the aforementioned
This time you spaced once again
It's easy to keep doing
But each time harder to stay sane
So find what you love
And be careful with all you find
You will learn that all wisdom
Comes from putting in the time
I know with this idea
The simple pleasures that are fast
Will become substantially menial
It takes great effort to make things last

TIMBER

Life seen through a shimmer
A shadow casts a spell
Fog suspends
As the moment bends
Encasing and embracing
All perfection.
There are a telling of secrets
Permeating existence
With a stillness
That through time
Has nourished and provided
Been patient and wise
Supported simplicity
In what is pure
While facing demise
Still, lending, to peaceful engagements
With rings of union
Supporting integrity
And presenting growth
While trying to endure…
Energy, alive
Abundant allure
Arms reaching with grace
Each a miracle of dimensions
Recycling necessity
Do I need to mention
That if blinded by the forest
One can fail to see the trees
We're in need of more special moments
It's everything so please
Radiate, Resonate,
Contemplate, Believe
In fate and don't ever wait
Or be to naive
To look into the beauty
That's left over from
What's not right

Cont.
In everyday life
Speak without bark
Be surrounded with vibrancies,
Visual, & Visceral,
Vicarious if need be
There is a needed voltage
Always current
And always connected
Always connecting
Branching out magic
Un focus, let go
Re-awake
Morph into
The space between
What can be seen
Beyond the physical
Wood you please
You're in fact
Already there

Figuratively trying to figure
The unfigurable
Is definitely indefinite

APPLY WITHIN

If you perfect what your passions are
While not necessarily trying to get very far
You may see favorable results, that are very real
I certainly do wonder, how a person does feel

About the concept and general spiel
Towards the need for a prolific career
It's ok to be consumed by something that has appeal
To you at least, and that's why you should steer

Your efforts towards any so called occupation
That is something that you so love to do
It may seem strange to create your own vocation
But at least then you know it's for you

Sometimes when we are trying just to make a living
At this thing known as the nine to five
Aim to figure out how much time you are giving
To the passions in life on that you thrive

When we end up not doing what gets us excited,
We may sell ourselves short, this I see
When things come easy do you tend to fight it
Certain endeavors that will always just be

The things that you will tend to do anyways
So you don't treat them like you would a profession
What would you really rather do every day
It's time you step up and make your confession

This life can become great, from the outside in
So having said this it's time to submerge
Not having given your real desires much time to begin
The results of any passions are enough to encourage

Cont.
Make this life grand from the inside out
By doing what it is that you really want to do
Because when doing these things you'll feel a certain clout
And a wonderful purity will come shining through

When there aren't any stares, who then needs to care
With how it is that YOU yourself feels
There are often so many expert opinions
That can have so much false appeal

Towards subjective accomplishments
Whose results will inevitably reveal
An enormous amount of outside attention
Why is status so often such a big deal

Please realize there is no need
To hold your breath
The job...or whatever you want to call it
I guarantee you it's already yours

On the next page is the original poem.
I had a tough time with this. First, after having left it for a month
or more I revisited it and thought that although I understood it, it
needed more clarity to be as poignant as I had intended. The flow
also seemed a little off. After a number of different times coming back
to it, the above result was revealed. At that point I went back to the
original and with one read through shook my head with a smirk as it
not only seemed to flow but made sense in the way I had originally
hoped it would.

You be the judge

APPLY WITHIN # 2

If you perfect what your passions are
While not really trying to get very far
You may see favorable results,
                        that are very real
I do wonder how this makes one feel
Towards the concept and general spiel
That seems to be trying to always make appeal
The need for a career, and the feeling of clout
Different from the passions we spend so much time without
While trying to make a living at the daily grind
We end up not doing what stokes us I find
And as life can become great from the outside in
Your real desires have had little time to begin
It's time to submerge into what you want to do
Because when you're doing what you want
A certain purity comes shining through
And when there aren't any stares
There's less relative care of other peoples beliefs.....
Well who needs to feel what you want to bequeath?
Why the attention of so much irrelevant appeal
About subjective accomplishment
Always such a big deal creating outside attention
Because you've achieved something worth a mention
There is no need to hold your breath
The job's already yours

TORTOISE HAIR

I wonder of where I'm going
Where I've been and where I'll be
I wonder of my direction
What I've seen and what I'll see

Things are certainly happening
But I feel a personal lull
Some things in life seem a constant struggle
Is the glass half-empty or is it half full

This is a question fore sure
That we all will come to face
Sometimes we just need to slow down
In order to win our personal race

TENURE

I can sense the possibilities
    BEYOND
        BEYOND
            BEYOND
The limiting boundaries of conceptualism
BEYOND
Passive expectations
BEYOND
Defined theories
That become excepted fact
BEYOND all stagnancy
Can we reach the ongoing creation
Of our own world?

STAKE YOUR CLAIM !

HUARAZ

Another passing rushing by
Looking through his own reflection
As the perfection
Of each field upon field
Radiating their yields
Show the way.
Secular integration
In a union that displays
Overall no real segregation
Mud huts, thatched roofs,
Clay brick abodes,
A plethora of worn hooves,
The smoke from wood stoves,
Llama, horse, alpaca, cow,
Chicken, lamb, a burrows brow
Raises in habit as we speed by
Sifting through the drifting clouds
The verdant landscape captivates
As an unhurried timelessness
Is freeze framed with turn of the head
The beautiful simplicities
Functioning precisely as they unfold
Just as I spy they do.
The dew glistens
To the necessity of its time
I find, what a recipe this does allow.
Tried and true
The blue of the beaming
Seemingly other worldly lupines
Transcend and lend to the vibrancies
Of the astute and oh so cute
Woman of the Peruvian highlands
Happy and hard core
Continuing on tradition
Emanating folk lore
Radiantly dressed
Minding their ways

Cont.

Occupied by the necessities
That we the western wicked
So often abuse and overlook
As I glance up to look
Out the window of my tour bus
I again catch my reflection
But this time it is
In the little boy
Wearing a red wool toque
And I am momentarily spooked
As I see myself
Walking joyfully a head of sheep
To a new pasture where they'll graze
I am always amazed
Where I find myself
As I remember that day
Turned back in time

HITCHING POST

It's a thumbs up trip
Self induced
A big mind fuck
You're chemically juiced
Floating along
As a convincing pretender
Sleighing the skies
Your head is a blender
Altering oddities to which you've surrendered
The "Best" times of your life
Will you even remember?
Please don't let this happen
Do grab a hold of your time
And realize that escape
Can become the master of mind

BUS STOPPED

I look up in a daze
Surrounded I'm dizzy
Everything is happening
10 th story cubicles stare out
Staring on
Another story unfolds
Is it bold to say
That we purposeless
Except in our own glory?

COME ODDITIES

So many maniacal provocations
Causing controversy at large
In this ever-growing concrete jungle
Who the fuck's in charge
Responsible for our downfalls
Is it fair to pass the blame?
It's certainly not an individual problem
Yet enough to drive one insane

PICKET FENCED

A fine line we walk
Trying to get a head
In our prescribed plethora of chaos
Based on what's read and said
Look into the eyes
There are a certain few
Glinting with Maddness / Genious
Which mania's becoming you

LONGEVITY

In the midst of it all
We sometimes let go
For one moment truly free
We live and we grow

True feelings and expressions
It doesn't seem real
Or is it? Only you know
That's existence you feel

This something do we all see
If so, why then so fast
Laughter, love, peace and humanity
Can't we make these things last?

QUIET ON THE SET

Would you be ever amazed
If you just happened upon your act
It may be hard to realize
When one has their back
Turned on themselves
Making it so easy to delve
Deep into the characters of discovery
But loving thee can become
A grey area in the plethora
Of contested hysteria
That may be created
While parading around
As a matter of fact extra

READY....AND ACTION

I dare you to become, who you are in your mind
I can guarantee you that now is exactly the time
To become whom you think is your ultimate you
Incorporate a consistency that can be so hard to do

Especially if you have an idea of the power of your being
To the point that it's again tomorrow you're seeing
As the day in which you will vastly re-arrange
It's just that easy when tomorrow you'll change

You know you can, you know you will, except you never do
The days go by and you get it on, when do you see things through
 It's easy in ones head sometimes, when to anything you can commit
Through this time though you are but who?...
                              and suddenly then that's just it

So live your potential, less from words more from action
Because only you can provide your internal satisfaction
It will take some time, but noble habits can firmly form
Making it easier to find smooth sailing.....
                              having ridden your personal storms

KNOCK KNOCK

The reality of your reality
Can eclipse your imagination
Which is an integration
And interpretation
Of really the same thing, isn't it?
Does that ring your bell

DUALITY

The mind beyond space
Is the last frontier
The more we seem to know
The more we seem to fear

Like when participating in a dream
And experiencing what you feel
Although you can stand back and simply observe
The two perspectives keep you in the surreal

Are you your own master?
Even when in this state
Or just a part of the whole
This leaves much to debate

The duality is mysterious
Are you always consciously at the helm
Probably not, but with some practice
You can be aware of more than one realm

IDEAS IDEAS

We're all just a good idea
Away from a better idea
On how to implement
Our ideas......
.......Just an idea I think

PIVOT POINTS

We've been given this time
It's a gift let me say
And this time's only now
So take charge in today

Don't pass up on experiencing
Even what's run of the mill
Keep happenings in context
Become who you will

Remembering anything you've taken
In the form of a pill for a thrill
Can be achieved with natural commitment
With no downside ~ what a skill

We must evolve and evoke internal change
While living in such a pivotal time
Don't become redundant and personally estranged
What are you prepared to lay on the line

Grab the bull by the horns
Please learn from what has past
We are on a crucial heading
That may or may not last

SCARED YET

Don't be afraid to make mistakes
But in the same
Definitely refrain
From making mistakes
Because you're afraid

JUST DO IT

Any job at hand
Could create other opportunity
But taking a stand
And seeing things through can be
A very hard task
However simple it may seem
You just have to ask
The person who has all the dreams
How much of each he ever gets to
What fun is there
In being the jack-ass
Of all trades
And the ace it seems of none
What will become
If the jobs at hand
Never get done?
Care to see

RISE AND SHINE

Steppin outa bed early
Instead of outa line late
Can make your strait hair curly,
The feeling is great.
What is your fate,
Written in stone?
Because of the way
In which you have been shown
This has more to do with who?
It's committing to choices, that makes you,
Well
You, Curly Q

RIGHT THEN

The end of order is chaos
The law upholds our fears
Perhaps a false sense of security
Without it do things seem less clear?

Drones caught in a conditioning
Governed to live like we do
Freedom is never a constant
As is the hesitancy to break on through

Subjective subconscious reality
What is right for you might not be for me
So many consumed by ignorance
It's ok to agree to disagree

Memories can become who we are
It is good to look back and see
What has worked and what has not
Recognizing who you don't want to be

RADIO HEAD

Imagine a rested mind
Staring at a radio
Listening to the fusion
Of sound waves
Binding with your illusions
That turn the page
Of synaptic interpretation
What intriguing elation
When looking at the speaker box
An letting your mind
Do so much more
Than the rest

CYCLEING

The magical snow tries to fall
The seasons try to change
The air begins to quietly chill
Then the snow turns back to rain

The Brilliance of the colors
As autumn passes through
Winter is nearly upon us
Soon summer for the roo

Opposite seasons
Yet still the same
Soon will come spring
Then summer again

With spring growth and revival
The buzz of the honey bee
With the heat spring blends to summer
We bear down and are truly free

These seasons represent a cycle
Always coming back to the start
This will certainly continue to happen
Even when from this life we part

RELEASE

I sneeze
You say "God Bless"
In hearing this I must confess
That if you do not
Acknowledge the powers that be
What will you see
No Unity?
Believe in this at least….
We need converge and submerge
Ourselves into the idea
Of all being (s) different
But yet the same
It's not plain nor simple
That's for certain
And in this curtain call
I will mention that a sneeze in fact
Is the closest biological sensation
Known to man
To mimic an Orgasm
Of coarse we Bless creation
When allowed
Such intriguing elation!

ADRIFT

Tugging @ my anchor of being
In my stationary drift
Tides ever changing
The rip and the pull take their toll
A distorted flow
Lifeless currents
Reflect an obscure chaos
The cleansing calm before the storm
Violently is disrupted
Will your anchor hold?
Restoration of self is sought
But who are you....
      Who are we....
          Who am I....
This restless cycle
Has no choice but to continue
As we thrash about
In our individual vessels

BEINVENIDO

Wind chimes
And base lines
Are carried away
In the foray
Of contrasts
The night holds
A bold allowance
In Cartegena
Tourist police
With their uni formed
Creased official slack
Gun ready for attack
On the chosen petty
Who with perfect consistency
Persistently loose sight
And in such slight
Disregard all consequence
That can be severe
Even thought they appear
To be removed
From actuality
When abused
To fatality
The senility
Of your touristic
Unrealistic, let loose state
Has innate consequences
The plastic fabrication
Of the presence for feeling
Isn't stealing the fact
That blatant corruption
Precludes the eruption
Of the fallacy of what you see
To be the mocking birds
Of a society
That should be respected
The fairytale streets

Cont.
The monumental defeats
That the city has become
To some is a free for all
Access, excess pass
That I hope doesn't last
Without admiration and respect
For the folk who still protect
An awareness that extends
Beyond the walls
That help lend
To one of the most
Welcoming places
Expressed by smiling faces
By all the folk
Who walk their paces
In every different regard
Yet accept that what is hard
Is what you may make of it
Hookers, coke lords, bankers
Foke lore, a bad global rap
For what? Keeping things in tact
Beyond the accepted insanity
Of a conditioned western world
Viva Columbia

POP TART NATION

We live entrenched
In a sexually drenched
Culture on the fence
Not sure of what sense
To make of the availability
Of dirty deeds
Sometimes causing senility
Done dirt cheap
What is it to meet
In the middle
I question who
May be messing with who
Have you been made
When strumming to the tune
Of your own three cord encore
In this orchestrated
Global sex machine
Hyphenated, often degraded
Revolt of Revolution
Make your own conclusion
If you're reading this
You're probably not
Going to loose
Your virginity again

OVERHEAD COMPARTMENT

Is your head
Your head
On your shoulders,
Only realized
By the eye of the beholders
Do you think what you feel
Are personalities you steal
Whose luggage is over your shoulder?
These questions I ask
Because when you're spread too thin
Things tend to be over before they begin
And it's a personal discovery when you come to your wake
And see things for what they are
Now there's less give and take
You see not much has changed
It all keeps ticking along
You've blinded yourself
Because you refuse to see wrong
And this quality some possess
Can rub off on their peers
Don't run off on yourself
Trying to keep your head clear

STAR DUST PAN

We are merely a parasite
In the spectrum of what we know
A parasite in itself
How far does reality go

The reality is
There really is none
No end to the mountains
No end to the sun

To think anyone knows
Anyone than they do
Is like a penguin flying high
Do you think that you know you

To think even at all
Can bring on a confusing blur
Be content just as a parasite
For we're far less in the big picture

THAT FEELING

Shedding another skin
An eroded continent
Wears thin its alluring layer
That a conveyor of evolution
Might say is just another solution
To my grain of sand theory
That I do query
In the desert of cosmic happenings
The wind sings its song
Picking up as it dances along
A chorus line from the beach
That will inevitably reach
Itself again, when it is
Displaced in its place
Not misplaced or erased
Just interlaced with necessity
Which always tends to be
What is, that that just is
Mimicking the off shore spray
The elements display
A quaint understanding
Of everything more
Or less demanding
At last there is no contrast
Between what is here to be seen
As harmonies moments.
Oh the bliss
Of dawn patrol
Strolling onwards
At the gesture of first light
All sensations sensational
Entirely just right
The day becomes you
With this merger
Of perfect alignment
The oceans taunting
Will often leave you
Wanting nothing more

REITERATION

A redundant voice
From a confused state
Deeply embedded
In that same place
That from when you did begin
There was nothing yet scrambled
Just very simply understood
And with time
What could be spoken
Had Actions lent
Without second thought
In the obvious
You're caught
When not followed
Through on
Care and wisdom
Again is sought
Over and over
Stupidity I've fought
It has its price
The mind deflects
And selects
What it is
It wants to hear
Steering clear
Of really listening
And that's pissing me off
I no longer care
To repeat myself
Did I defeat myself
I repeat to myself
Did I repeat myself
Again? I repeat

EMMA

The long shadows
Bring the warmth of the day
To a momentary stand still
As my fill
Of tranquility
Whispers to the horizon
This perfection
Speaks softly
Of everything that is good
And as the sun's glow moves on
I know while it's gone
That your sparkle
Will help illuminate all
As your light
Ups the constellations

COMPLETER

I search through all tranquility
For a gentle expression
That like you
Transcends understanding
And understood thought
Speechless I succumb
To my own absolute
A newfound contentment
With purpose and time
Magically calms
Through your divinity
My spirit is lifted
Emanating all purity
I thank you for your help
In manifesting unity

SLOW BURN

Oh my
Oh my love
It's getting to be…
Oh so so,
Oh so late again
Where has your path
Woven you?
I've been waiting,
Well kind of
I've been doing some things
Like gaining on life
And understanding
Through strife
That all things demanding
Lend to forever,
Please come in
My friend
My future
My past
Wisdom I send
A true cure
To all that last
I've kept the flame aglow
Seek refuge and know
Everything
It's real
Oh my
Oh my love

INCORPORATION

From the deepest place
In my most thought out being
With an infusion of grace
I am finally seeing
What I've known
For so very long
But now looking back
Realize I have seldom shown
And to continue on
With a truthful pride
I must incorporate
A committed stride
It's long past essential
While more understood
To realize any potential
A proud cadence should
Be consistent with my knowing
And persistent with me showing,
Coinciding with what I do
These qualities need be,
Always followed through on
But with growing can come latching
To certain things that are now gone
And in my own consistent inconsistency
It's easy to wonder about what went wrong
Although seemingly enough ahead
In other peoples eyes
Am I becoming easily read
This could cause a slow demise
You see I often tend to stumble
And there is this grumble
Of time, it's getting louder
I am finding
Sustaining not just confidence
But competence
Can be confusing

Cont.

In who you are
Is how you are
How are you....
Is how you do
How do you do?

LISTEN HEAR

Your speak has purpose
Your speak has flow
There's rarely surplus
You seem to always know
The message you send
You're always thought out
You consistently lend
Without any doubt
Your clarity and view
An open-mindedness
That is so very you
And in understanding
With your voice
That life is inevitably
Affected by all choice
You have experience
And a committed direction
And I am very blessed
To receive your affection
I so value my friend
What you have to say

MASTERPEACING

I leap and I laugh
Together with the cosmos
Orbiting above the earth
Soaring free
With each dancing breath
As the untaught symphony
Of existence
Unfolds before me
Enveloping all that is
Sometimes swallowing whole
Spontaneous fantasia
Leaving organized ignorance;
My chosen path is still unmarked
As the winds of my laughter
Help carve my unconditioned direction

The contemplation equation
Is the tightening grip on frustration
Ousting any emancipation
Causing a global stalemate
In our salvation

HUMANS BEING

We rarely give permission
To ourselves
In this day
To be fantastic
And I am truly wishing
That with the elves
We all could play
To be enlightened
From this human condition,
That can be hell
To keep at bay
The compounding of profanities
Surrounding our modern day
Is a fast track to insanity
That is creating so much disarray
We need to nurture
What's left in humanity
Let the conditioning go
Grow through the absolute
In between form and opinion
Is your imorternity

I FOLD

The lines
We've crossed
YELLING
Shut your trap
When you're talking to me
Why don't you have any tact
Why do things seem to be
            So Wrong?

Put your rusty sword away
I've done the dishes…
And my steel wool
Is now tossed
Like my wishes
Fragmenting down the drain

Your half empty glass
Will never quench
Your crass
Mordant, redistilled spew
Languages
That you don't even understand
Seem more appealing to you

Less to interpret
Your figuring
Is blind
You're are the cats ass alright
Flaunting your tail all the time

You forget that you pretend
And pretend to forget
There was so much
That I loved in you
And in some ways I let

Cont.
The stray momentary passion
Became something
That without intent,
Or thought, or even consciousness
Circled like a vulture
Waiting to feed on the weak

While pretending to soar
Believable for seconds
But gravity prevails
Taking its toll
Consequently
It wasn't grounding

Your lies and insecurities stole
Trust, love and nobility
Belief, purpose and soul
Worth, honesty and effort
All those things
That make one feel whole

Knowing the difference
Between right and wrong
Is nothing without action
And without any doing,
Before long

What you know
In your head
Becomes removed
From what
Is shown

Why does
Intellect become
So secondary
When the coup
Has been flown

Cont.
With clipped wings
Your purpose is blown
You can no longer glide
And the boring routine
Festers with all that is mean

You want the full nest
You had before
Convinced you can control
All of what's in store

Yet the nest is permanently shaken
Soon to be overtaken
You finally realize
That playing games
Will never result in a winner
When the games involve peoples hearts

A queen doesn't deserve to be jacked around
And the king played as the joker from the start
Will demolish a full house
And put the fold
On your soul
Regardless of intentions
You end up reaping
What you sew

If you happen to be ever fucked over
There may be a message
That is lent
It will stay
With you forever
And help honesty
Make a little more sense?

Cont.
It's all simple
As can be
Without explanation
Understood
So why the Christ is it so hard
To behave always how you should

Trying to protect others from your shortcomings, is inevitably energy
Focused with skewed intent.

REDUCED RECYCLED REUSED

There are implications absurd
When relating to one individuality
Can't each voice be specifically heard
Like Run Lola Run…..
Do you see what I see?

We are made up of molecules
From the inside and out
That have all been somewhere before
This is something, that without any doubt
Relates directly to the every things core

In our illusion of constant permanence
Essentially even our minds will be reduced back to dust
We want to feel safe and create a tangible world
But full circle is the only true thing we can trust

We're subordinate to our limitations
Always keeping us who we are
Do we not realize the dynamics of progress?
We must slow down and simplify
Or we'll never get far

MODERNITY GRITY

Accepted by most
With little thought
Lest to boast
Is our role
As so-called intellects
Feeling appalled I dissect
The human race
What an upper echelon
Pandemic disgrace
It's over....all
That we claim superior
But the oh, so so
So very inferior?
Homo sapient
Has self proclaimed rational thinking
So many captaining this ship
That with humanity is sinking
And greed can keep one driven I see
But being greedy
Well that's a given to me
It will crush what is pure
Being greedy has no cure
There's always more
Until there's less
And with depletion no doubt
There is a global undress
It will just take longer
For the so called stronger
With no integrity and false moral
We seem to be governed
By heartless mongers
Who I think should all be corralled
Silver spooners
To whom we give power

Cont.
Closer by the second
To the deciding hour
Why do we continue
To choose
The purpose ignorance
Of modern man

GAPETTO

I gasp grasping
To the edge
Of my breath
Is this water oxygenated
I wonder what is fated
As the slaughter
Of another tree falls
In a forest so deaf
To the ears
Of the puppeteers
Cinching the strings
Around the ring
Of the last contenders

BREAKING TRAIL

Followers we are
Uncharacteristically beaten
The path is such
We can forget our way
To search
WE search
It's an infinite search
Never defined nor definite.
Seizing imagination
We selectively Integrate
Manifestation
Subjective and rejective
Positively negative
The path wears on
As do we all
Inevitably consumed
The mind, the body
Even the soul
Do we ever find
We're ever whole
Are you ready
Holding steady
Is this who we are
Are we all of this
Evolution
Revolution
Institutions
Conclusions
Few stray
To many pray
We don't utilize
What's realized
Who Empathizes
With challenging fear
Live while you can
Mastermind a plan
Lend a hand

Cont.
Love and be loved
Follow your heart
Not the beaten path

SURROUNDED

When it's all said and done
The things that matter most I see
Are not the size of any accomplishment
But the people that are apart of me
......be careful in this,
They just may go hand in hand......

DIGGING DEEPER

With our encompassing nature
Nature itself
Is being overthrown
What we've known
For a very long time
Is now a song and dance
That ya you fancy pants
Can no longer ignore
We are on a collision course
With ourselves
Soon to be floored
How long will we pretend
To ignore the ultimate factors
Which will forever be
A sore spot for all to bear.
The access to commodities
Like water is evaporating
Sparing a very few
Who know what and how to do,
Like the essentials of growing provisions
They may be fortunate enough
To pull through what decisions
Are you making to help
There is no mistaking these words
Soon certain occupations
Very well might seem absurd
That tend to be respected
Perhaps to much today in this world
I should say, they may become meaningless
I confess with no intent for ill regard
It is just becoming so very hard
To take care of necessity for so many
It's uncanny that we need to infect
Everyone with this understanding
That we can no longer stall
In our re organization and deliberations

Cont.

Before the downfall ensues
It will then be true for all
The importance of getting enough food
And not to sound rude
But the people with skills
Not just to pay the bills
But to produce, yes produce
Will stand atop of the hill
Everything in comparison
Will instantly loose its value
Making malleable analysis
Useless... blow your profession
A kiss goodbye
Unless you can derive
Sustenance in traditional ways.
These days are numbered
As we blunder along
I hope more to recognize
The sobering thoughts
Instead of being righteously caught up
In that it will never happen to me
It is don't you see
There is such little regard
For our water or even land.
The only stand needs to be a stand off
These problems aren't a hiccup
As I cough under my protective mask
What tasks of survival can YOU really perform?
Soon most will be naturally a re course
In this resource depleted war torn planet
We are manic in our ways
With our politicians and bankers
Hankering for the last laugh
The wankers and all their staff
Including most of the contemporary population
That had no foresight or even contemplation
About the aforementioned ramifications

Cont.
And their essential re-inventions
Will create a reverse dissention
In the ranks of the overly modern, modern man
Brinking the span of a new intellectual superior
That will afresh the knowledge
Of producing sustenance one again
Coming to the light the inevitable end
Of all jumbo jets and Mercedes Benz
Seeing the virtue in the farming folk
And the holistic ways, it's not a joke
What will rule will not be cash flow
But crops you know, practical skills
That no one can really go without
I doubt litigating over these facts
Will fly when the runways are all closed
A radish will be of more value
Than the rubbish of currency
Time to get gardening
It's really quite grounding

W

You can't discuss the future
With the people who have none
I feel the need to cuss at you sir
What a president you did become

Conspiracy theories,
Return points passed
You re-write the legislature
Just to make your chosen wars last

The tsunami in the pacific
Nuclear testing gone awry?
Just some minor population control
How many of "your" people die

Fighting for commodities
And resources that soon will be
Tapped, depleted, and sucked right dry
Open your fucking eyes and see

That humanity is suffering
On every inch of our fragile globe
While you are responsible for killing sprees
From your oval office you call an abode

How do you rest you your murky soul
How are you not haunted every night
How do you consider your dignity whole
You're so far beyond fight or flight

You're in a bush league of your own

THE BLACK HOUSE

For a long while
With many a superficial smile
"Prolific Specialists"
Who were mere pawns enlisted
Specifically gifted responsibility
To put societies at ease
While politicians are screaming
Please please please
It's of no worry
As they scurry away
To their not so common seats
Behind closed doors
Dragging their feet
At a pace that can be ignored
No more.
Industrial pollutants
It's an acute reality
Fakers, takers, policy makers
Must recognize our lies
While bordering no return
Are we learning that it's all
Or nothing, cussing won't bring
The levels of methane
Down to a sane level
We revel in our "intellect"
As the Patchamama
Continues to collect
In her puzzled gaze
A burdening haze
Of carbon dioxide
And chlorofluorocarbons
So very hard on us all
Combining with nitrous
Stalling the ensuing implosion
In order to fight this
We need act now
Let's keep things in tact

Cont.

For our continental shelf
Is so much more important
Than our continental self
Eating our continental
Mental breakfasts
While quickly approaching
Our breaking point break
Induce wise action
The satisfaction is long lived
In the proper doing
Lets pick the mental grid lock
The combination Barack
Is in your chest pocket

PRIME SINISTER

The pervading elicitation
Of every detail
A missed invitation
To an illicit pre sale
Of all of our streams
Our memories and dreams
The creams of our crops
Are curdling away
While in dismay
Mouths are left unfed
What happened to the notion
And devotion
Of equality
In our daily bread
Eh Man
Apparently Harpering away
Will leave us high and dry

HOLD PLEASE

With peak production
The level of suction
Towards extinction
Is at a powerful brink.
Fun is the act
But keeping things in tact
Means we must admit
To the facts not just sit
And attack from afar
All in favor
Of the checks and balances
Not the cheques
That are balance less
Our prime defect
Is with a blinding malice
We forge ahead
And it has to be
Not just said
With isolated whispers
In denial tones
We need a honed
Action plan in action
How many Mr. Smiths
Can the operator handle
With jumbled lines
I find catastrophe
To be approaching
Encroaching so fast
We'll just have to see
Who and what
Will be to last
Realizing the joke
Is no joke
Is on us
Oh Extinction
What's the fuss
All these "trends"

Cont.
Can be mended
If not reversed
If not, oh well
The universe
Will certainly abide
Yeah that's right dude
Oh what a ride it's been
Taking its own round side
While keeping stride
With her survival
Precedents have been set
Who's on hold now

*NOTE:

I make reference to the Smiths as a common name in regards to all people being equal, not a singling out of a single person with a certain title. The operator is in fact the earth mother, somehow, barely, still holding it down in our destructive wake.

1 PLUS 1

An internal battle of forces within
A self inflicted struggle, let the games begin
Stubborn behavior, un resolving at best
Some specific issues should just be left to rest

We must agree to disagree
Helping preserve our individuality
Although we have formed a bond as one
It is still yourself that I hope you become

I ask: is the functioning of my body intertwined
With the mind? Is there a bind...
Or are they separated,
Isolated, never mated, alienated
What movements are re-created
When we manage to hit rewind
Exacerbated conflict I find
Externalize a sacred balance
Please lend all necessities
To this crucial time

HAMMOCKA

I lay here and swelter
In the heat of my thoughts
I am still amongst the movement
Rocking to and fro
Wondering in the heat
Have all the lullabies vanished me
Turn back a page
Maybe a chapter or two
And remember again
When you knew nothing.
Everything comes
Full circle

SOAKED HIGH BROW

The air of enchantment
Wafting in subdued rushes
Luscious is the silence of colour
The smells of everything
So familiar yet indescribable
The pollinating air will
Have you engulfed
You become an ism
While momentary synergism
Carries you away
With the winds and scents
Of the dissolving midday heat

TACKALONE

A personal journey
An eternal quest
All to find out
For you what's best.
In this physical realm,
What is real
Who's at the helm
How do you feel
Are we bailing an ocean
If so can you swim
Where does the water end
And where does it begin
For this there's no answer
To each their own
Does the ocean get bigger
Or smaller
The more oats that are sewn?

BALANCING ACT

Living over the top
In your head
Elevated
Super star status
In a world you created
Is the projection
Necessary?
For the manifesting
To carry
One for so long...
The mental preparation,
It helps to belong
In an untrue reality
Waiting for your queue
Why live in this fallacy
That is no doubt very skewed?
It's what so many seem to do
When's the time to confess
What a mess you've created
While avoiding your best
No longer elevated,
Still dressing the part
With so many skills acquired
Where do you start
With the people who inspire?
What are you prepared to see through
Start looking inward
For the clearest view
Are you well versed
In adversity
While living free
Helps you to know
Who you don't want to be
As you grow
Your consistency
Helps create
A clean slate

Cont.
And with no debate
Gaining independence
Can bring with it pain
As you begin to mend
Over time it's plain
To see that you are not
Someone else's guilt
That you once built
A life with
Your gift is you
While courage
When blue
You deserve
To be cherished
Always
It's not fair if
Your commitment
Falls away
Unnoticed
Unbalanced
Unappreciated
With malice
Why does love complicate
It doesn't have to
Depreciate
While you contemplate
How another
Can't wake up
To reciprocation
Of simple elation
Trust, nurture
And continued creation
Of a once beautiful union
That looking back on
And now seeing
Through and through

Cont.
Was based as much
On perceptions
With deflections
Of admittance
The inevitable good riddance
Should have happened
Long before
But when things were great
The obvious,
It came on slow
In your mind and your heart
All you wanted to know
Was what?
Was capable
Blind with confusion
About the illusion
Of love
Dissecting and protecting
Insatiable for perfecting
Now time for reflecting
And from what you've learned
You won't again get burned
Magic is possible
A balanced relationship
Unstoppable
With encouraging, equal
Respect, flourishing
What you seek well,
It is......
Being realized

YOU'RE TIME

Try to allow a little blank time
Every single day and in this
I hope you may find
That however these moments
Happen to be spent
That this time is lent
Exclusively to you
And what you may do
Is outright yours to see through
Sometimes a bit
May tend to get wasted
But that's juts it in the end
Not a relative term
In this one can learn
Just how much indeed
That you can get done
When not on the consummate run
In the span of two hours
More perhaps I laugh
When you are empowered
Than the entire previous 2 months
Sometime it's ok to bunt
Rather than swing for the fence

CAPT'N DAN

Steele arms of rapture
I see horizon bound
The peaceful sound
Of a grumbling evolution
Eroding through a translucent flow
Determined necessity
Survival is no longer free
Encroaching, Poaching
Depletion approaching
An opening is closer
To a permanent closure
When the sea is baron then....
What, point did we erase simple care
For the mother of all
At any costs we are catching
Ourselves as we delve
Deeper, it's darker
No more resource
Past the point of recourse
Our safety nets are far too frayed
With off course bearings
Our luxuries tangle with illogic
As we winch in the lines of despair
We must care for more
If we're to have anything in store
Beyond another 5 course spiel

ENCORE

A vulnerable pull
Helps make full
My insecurities
Towards the relations
And summations
Of the unions
That creation it self
Was not unaware of
But pure care for love
Didn't manifest
Until after
The frill
Wilted,
Flooded; a disaster
My fill silted
Now empty
Moving faster
Trying to catch up
To missed takes
What's in security
When sometimes faked
Craving maturity
Realizing which voices
Need to be heard
Do I need to set the stage
With a fresh actor?
Or is that absurd
There's no audition
To understanding
Maturities part
With substance
And sustenance
Taking center stage
I will soon reveal
Who will steal
The leading role
In one final love story

OH BABE

The baby in me
Curious as can be
Is growing and free
And with regression I see
That most all is perspective
But when rejected
We're all affected
Then insecurities again
Become known
Leaving my mind
One more time blown
Because I have been shown
More than everything.
Through observation
& contemplation
Of now understood mistakes
Followed by heart breaks,
For heavens sake....
The toll is taken
And although aching
I am closer to myself
But so far away
From my baby
There is no maybe
What I feel is everything
There is nothing less
I confess to have learned
In this race, application
In setting free Love
Always to be contemplating
What is elating
Can blur clear thought
I ought to know
What I feel
In your glow
It's taken forever,
Oh the mind so clever

Cont.
Refrain is necessary when
Trying to dissect and project
Always wanting to re-direct
Forever is now
After and before
Leaving whatever's in store
Just beyond the shore;
Patience; we need more,
Without clutching
Because such a thing
Sometimes automatic
Can flip side
And even when turned
Upside down
Real Love can't hide
Or always be understood
But felt and known
Developed and shown
Baby oh baby

FLOATING THE NHILE

A sudden super charge
Of nihilistic emotion
Or had it crept up from a place
That had since been stripped
Of any devotion
Noticed dissipation
Of the joy for all creation
Why become this haunting
Of diabolic melancholy
The invasion perhaps
A creation of the mind.
Minding this helps when
Pointing to the abyss

CLASS 5

The torrents of thought
In the river of mind
A back eddy is sought
Yet the momentum I find

Carries me away
With a turbulent pull
Getting churned, the disarray
Is like a stampeding bull

Yet this rodeo's in your head
And for calmer water you pray
This thinking doesn't need to be fed
Go with the flow of the day

TAKING FLIGHT

You recognize choice
Giving the voice
In the back of your mind
A solidified Identity
And this I see to be you
Your oh so sweet sound
Your even sweeter soul
Every eve of your being
It is everything so whole
And everything is you
You own your becoming
So now become your own
It's not a slip stream
Behind your chosen dream
It's your reality dear
I hope you're making now
The time to soar

BOLING POINTS

Dealing with hate
Through hatred
Is a pot calling
The kettle black
We need to let go
Of our proving grounds
And not be so ready to attack
It takes courage to always nurture
When neurosis seems more the norm
But this is always when love is needed the most
Allow your deepest connections to be reborn
All of life's pre-conceptions
Tend to harden ones soul
Try to stay caring, open and kind
These qualities will help one to grow

MAGIC MAKER

I'm convinced that you are magic girl
Or maybe just a magician at heart
I'm pretty sure you know psychogeneses
Because you've been moving me right from the start
From the very first day I was graced with your presence
Time in my life seemed to somehow stand still
My whole world changed, my reality re arranged
The impossible was defeated
...........and my dreams were eloquently filled

TELL ME MORE

I hope you are told
Ten times a day
Words that should never get boring
Keeping one soaring,
Never to fade away.
Told and shown
Love is bold and must be grown
I hope you do hear
This often My dear
With or without me
I hope always
Your eyes and ears
Are blessed with and see
I love you
I love you
I love you...
And know love's an action
Not simply just a word
And in conjunction with now
It would be totally absurd
If you haven't already seen
And certainly heard
So many times this day
Already and again
And again, I can't refrain
I'm ready.....to love you
And you thought show and tell
Was just for kids

REUNION

I remember a night
That I remember floating
I remember a light
That from me was glowing
It was commented on
By an old friend
Who was so radiant herself
She said "it's nice to meet you again,
Your aura looks so vibrant,
You're overflowing with everything good"
It was simply being in your presence
That I hope was understood.
You make me believe in enchantment
It's your energy that captivates
The words it's nice to meet you again
Are certainly ones
To which I can relate.....
　　　　......I've missed you

Flirting with thee:
Certain mind structures
Certainly can fuck your ability
To let go of ego

FINAL VERDICT

Do we make It
In the end
How so
So easy
I lend this perspective
About passing the buck
Judgment
It's so fucked
Usually when?
Yes....
Usually then
At our worst
We tend to nurse
The curse of dwelling
The profound thing
Is not what; I ask
You are dealt
But how you feel,
How you felt
How you think
When at the brink
About thinking
Next time
There may be just
So much more
Says the encore
Of a time worn man
Than his saunter
Down easy street
How will we make it
In the end

SPARKS

What captivates
More passionately
Than the flame of connection
While the shadows dance
There is a spiritual affection
The mystic, the romance
Everything in between
The pleasures and pain
Again and again
The trickery of senses
Inexplicably defenseless
As the entrancing flicker
Sometimes slowing
Sometimes quicker
Radiates dimensions
With no intentions
Other than to please
Sizzling, wet, soothed
Dizzying, sweat, moved
Basking, not asking
Knowing and glowing
In the spellbinding light
Of your mesmerizing form

.

SIGN SEAL AND DELIVER

When things come round again
As they always do my friend
What rotation will you be on
Catching up to life's cycle,
Before another is gone?
Off axis I feel
While the same lessons I steel
My plans seem to be real
But getting there, well
Always such an ordeal
How come
You don't come around
Any more
Did the revolving existence
Start becoming a bore
What if things
Don't come around
In the end
So many messages
I have
Ready to send
Personal delivery
I do recommend
Licking stamps is far too risky

TEN FOOT POLE

Your Diss Stance
Seethes me
Stirring the cauldron
Of confrontation
I have proved
To be worse
Such a reactive
Instinctual curse
Getting sucked in
To your vortex of superiority
It's a heaving facade
A front up front
Hiding fragility
Causing senility
Keep your ground please
You Poser

COVER ME

The choices we create
For heavens sake
We must make
For our protection
A clear direction
With give and take, allows reflection
About the life we've been given
Are you really livin, or are you caught
In the big siv.....and
Just straining as you go, against the flow?
If so, I'll have you know
That you do belong,
Keep keeping on
We must set ourselves free
Please let the positivity
Swallow me, swallow you
Help us through
Envelope whole
Ya we develop as we go
Sometimes practical,
Sometimes theatrical
Fuck factual, what's actual
Is different in the same
Cover my back will you
What is engrained
From the start,
It's not a game
And my heart
No longer played
Makes me say
It's getting plain
To see
What I need
I feel creed
With your love
Together, tighter
Lifted up, forever brighter
Your needs become me

HE'S GOT THE LOOK

It appears unanimously
I bore the look of a local
Wondering not so much
How to digest this focal point
The fact usually is
I continue laughing
While showing tact
Blending in while standing out
In the same lines
I am reminded
Of satire, oh the quagmire
Of the echoing song
Karma chameleon
Stealing identical moments
Time frames time
And I find no harm
In feeling like you belong
It helps when you're W'ron

DANCE FLOORED

The dance floor evaporates
Preceding the beat
You become symbiotic sound
There is nothing else
I see
I feel
I sense
I hear
Your resonance
Soothed by your gentleness
I am transfixed in your dimension
The sensation of a butterfly kiss
Is always worth a mention
Get a room someone yells
Yeah more room...
It broke the spell
Excuse me sir
Are you leaving soon
With you gone
We'd have more room
More room to move
More room to groove
Room to let go
And room to sooth
With instinctive being
Eyes closed still seeing
Creating a flow
As you again let go
Your synergism is contagious
You help make music glow
Enveloped by your warmth
I notice the jealous man
Slowly slinking away

MERGE

WITH EVERY BREATH
I ENHALE YOUR BEAUTY
GLEAMING, I FEEL ELECTRIC

YOU HAVE HELPED ME
FEEL THE CONTENTMENT
OF A COMPLETEST
MY FEELINGS HAVE VENTURED
TO PLACES NEVER BEFORE FELT

UNAWARE
UNTIL YOU'RE AWARE
AND EVEN BEFORE IT WAS SOMETHING
THAT YOU MAY HAVE ALREADY KNOWN

YOUR EXTAORDINARY DEPTHS
BLEND WITH MINE
TO FORM US AS ONE

MORE OR LESS

We carefully, egotistically, deliberately
Individually, foolishly construct
What inevitably more times than not
Is beyond a right fucked view
Of us in and on the world.
Most often scientific,
Boasting the prolific sate
Of our reduced, recycle, pre cycled, reuse
Absorbed, to used, confused
Perspective in our astute
Selective intellectual dissection
Of this ever going perplexion
That we really really know
We know more or less
Less than nothing about

RECOGNIZE

My wanderlust
Has thrust me
Into the unknown
Where
Am I left; I am left…
With the core
Of raw truths
Without seeds
There is no youth
What fruits of our labor
Can we savor for our young
What is to become
As we decimate
As we desecrate
We need to clean the slate
Peeling away layers
I feel a shedding
With heavy hearted tears
Though my heading endures
My skin is not so thick, I see
These lessons I picked
And now will be
Strengths observed
In weakness again
The crystal of clarity
Is a uniqueness that lends,
It's the same in everyone
Easily defined
Differently applied
Let me refine, lovingly
By your side
What happened to humanity
Why are so many off side
Inconceivable unfoldings
Speeding along
Alone again does anyone belong
In this inflicted chaos

Cont.

What a recognized pain
Distracted inclinations
Leaves me again
Confined and ram shackled
Yet ready to tackle
All internalization
While practicing elevation
I'm baffled
By a straightened smile
Aching for purity
Your radiance sooths
Lend me your light
Tapped and overflowing
You are glowing
Help melt away
All frozen anxiety
While releasing my captivity
From spiritual pain
I have envisioned my absolute
Why is sacrifice to be challenge
If it means more time from your self
I can't pinpoint the crucial moment
But it happened
I know myself again

WHOLE LOTTA LOVE

The elixir of life
Can't be found in a potion
It's not a mixture of words
Casting a spell into motion
It's essential to being
And can make fantasy so real
When the butterflies awake
That's perfect existence you feel
Although not found in one form
Of it you can't take a picture
There is no one certain meaning
Hidden in some ancient scripture
You can't buy it or sell it
Although some people do try
It amazes me to think
Without it a life could pass by
You can't hold it or smell it
But yes indeed it can bee seen
You're either apart of it or not
There's not much in between
The poor can be made rich by it
The rich can't do without
It can't be taken, borrowed, or begged
Rather consciously given out
It can be harmed not treated right
And can take some time to mend
It's not to be ever taken for granted
For this certainly bring nearer the end
What I speak of helps time make sense
And at times with your breath, may be taken away
Although always powerful beyond control
You should never keep it at bay
The elixir I speak of is unconditional
Always compassionate, caring and kind
It can be in the form of a friend with open arms
Or a smile even seen by the blind

Cont.
Forever remember that it's essential to life
Keep this in mind if ever push comes to shove
Always remember please how delicate things are
We must respect & cherish, always with LOVE !

YOU KNOW YOU KNOW

When nurtured and nourished
Perfection can be improved
Only then do thing flourish
Oh my......
Hearts you have moved
I so cherish our eternal becoming

ENGINE EAR

The shift of mood
I fear I hear
As the darkest hour
Before dawn stalls
Everything appalling
Usually subsiding
While this ride
Roller coasters
A loop to loop
Of chosen delight
And I divulge
In the light of the new day

It takes effort to represent a façade
Which seems quite peculiar and odd
When that effort could be better used
For choosing not to hide
behind any intentional fraud

93

SPELLBOUND

So alive
The passion of being
Enthralled by the moment
Overwhelmed by the possibilities
Elusive perfection lingers
An enigma of wonder
That you helped create
A new direction
The same destination
Floating along as one
Intentions and imaginations
Beyond our control
Impossible conflict
Can create it's own
The continuity of sustenance
In which I feel
Instinctive security
Memories of who we are
Resulting in what we know
Certain uncertainty
Trying to reason with emotion
No logical answers
What is real is real
I am spellbound
In your presence

TOTALITY

Got a whole bunch of incense burning
The smell reminds me
Of for something I'm yearning
Tomorrows always here.... I hear
Before the next day spawns
So many things that do confuse me
But certainly make me strong
Everyday we evolve
Everyday we become
Better for others
Worse for some
Will time catch eternity
And if so how come
If so many never feel
What it's like to be one
You are my rainbow
You're the sun that makes me shine
With you the word eternity
Means not enough time

SAULITUDE

In his primal self
He floated along
With a smile on his face
He helped us belong

Always gentle and kind
His laws written from heart
Good in us all he would find
And from us he'll never part

Saul was centered and balanced
Harmonious and kind
So content with his purpose
Ultimate peace he did find

95

TICK TOCK DOCK

Disposability abounds
With backwards
Leaps and bounds
In a temporary world
Ruled by funny money
Hounds sniffing buts
Kissing ass
Lacking nuts
Passing by
Passers by
On the fly
At a hundred million miles/hr
Where have all the wizards gone
It's wrong not to re-set
The metroGnome
Please Sir Cadium
Knight me proper
Slow things down
What talent
I wonder
Could be more
Extraordinarily important

REALEYES

The hollow pain
Constantly looming
I created it
Hindsight is inevitable

The emptiness lingers
So many mistakes
Your eyes find closure
Memories prevail

Your confidence crumbles
Insecurities come marching in
Now aware of this reality
The choice was mine

Defeat is overwhelming
Instant re-evaluation
Expect the unexpected
What matter has changed

Never take for granted
Cherish what you have
Realize love
Live it with praise

The scrambled confusion
Sometimes makes sense
If you decide to let it
Acquire forgiveness

YOU AGAIN

An echo in the valley of tears
Pierces the silence
Of my formless placeless being
Defiled by love
You hold captive my desires
I see in the murky waters of my emotion
And as I dive deep
Your reflection...... it disappears,
While exploring the depths
Of this pain and conflict
What can we expect;
To become, to be calm, to be whole
Do we deceive ourselves
While trying to nurture
All that seems pure and true
You radiate quality and virtue
And illuminate spirit
Yet I feel profoundly vulnerable
Re-surfacing I am filled
With your vibrancies
I recognize and feel the warmth
That is cast by your soul
This warmth is you

FOOLS GOLD

What are needs really?
Our needs
Are to live freely
With purpose and grace
Infused into everythingness
Yet with a glimpse into time
Looking through
To get through
I see a passing unaware
A passage with no care
We can't ignore despair
Unbeknownst as the fool
We tick on
Wound up
Ticked off
A half empty cup
What becomes revelation?
In an instant
We can awake
What is creeping and seeping
Up unto and out of
Your conscious being
What are you fleeing
Integrate consistency
This I see can prevent
Being blinded
By fools gold
In such superficial
Conditioned backwardness

LIP SYNCRO

Have we lost our place
For greatness, what disgrace
You can't debate this
In our consumed chase
With the big brass ring
The talent, any talent?
It tends to elude
"You can't even sing"
I Risk sounding rude
We've demolished any infrastructure
To support righteous purity
What I see, and what you hear
Will now forever be
And this I fear
The very superficial
Media created
Duped, artificial
Corporately paraded
Big boy bands
Bad girls taking stands
Fake wrinkled tans
And asinine implants
Created worlds
That are instant
Take a stand
Before we all hurl
Ourselves into
The mindless masses
How fast can you blow
A kiss Goodbye
Pucker up and pass
This encore
Onto your talent agent

REPEAT OFFENDER

If the best offence
Is indeed defense
Then in my defense
I may say
The opposite
May make sense
No offence
But in defending
My offence
Which has been on
It has shone
And perhaps
Come and gone
My timing wasn't off
My timing helped
Me to belong
In the craze
Of all craziness
That is best served
In less offensive
Smaller portions

DECIEVED

Another grey morning
Yet the skies are vibrant blue
The storm inside my head
Is depressing through and through

It's not even a self-induced state
From an unbalancing act after the fact
From abusing ample substance
Always adding to what's not in tact

Nope, this is just sober reality
And looking back it's not hard to see
That I've whittled away my securities
In an attempt to feel more free

And now I am scared and realize
That I have to start in some ways again
And I am not so much frightened by the challenge
I just don't know where to begin

Putting all your eggs in one basket
Unless they are all boiled hard
Especially when the basket isn't even yours
Can leave your eggs broken and in part

There may be others partially at fault
But you're inevitably the one to blame
For not choosing better partners
These chickens will soon go up in flames

Poisoning all with their influenza of lies
They use people to take their fall
Pretending to actually give a shit
These cocks need a wake up call

Cont.

But then again I guess so do I
I recon we reap what we sew
I'm done being taken advantage of
There's only one direction to go

And with the winds of change
The grey mourning of weather or not
Wisps away my clouded mind
And helps me see the opportunities I've got

GOOD THEN

A pulsing bliss
Skipping beats
Wondering how
My complete
Can be found
In the curtails
Of being.
Paradoxically
Strengths
And insecurities
Can erode purities
That appear
To be less
Than ubiquitous
In a pure state
We're all forming
Connecting connections
Beyond perfection
It's what I feel right now
Release and believe
That too good to be
Can prove to be true
Did it not happened
To me and to you?

INFILTRATION 102

Being aware of
With wholesome care
And attention to the moment
With slow sent messages
Of understanding, lending to
The absorption fully
Of the present
A gift that is lent
Through the now
Inoculate your immediate
State into everything vital
Getting settled
With un setting sights
Letting enlightenment
Represent through and through
Don't try to penetrate reality
You may end up sided
Down turned and burned
While deviating to fallacy
When instead you could be fed
By letting reality penetrate you

SYNAPSE

Oh how quickly
Our cerebral weather
Counts change
An electrical burst
Thoughts re arranged
A vortex of defense
In the cortex so dense
We sometimes fail
To instill witness
Of the currency
That controls
We need be whole,
Not clouded
With thundering jest
Keeping a breast
The winds of torment
That tend to blow away
Any reserved stillness
In the crispness
Of our temperate minds

Communicating essence
A synchronistic lesson
With nothing imposed
What you know
Is the presence
Of everything
Unwrapped, untapped
Exact

TUNED

When on your personal throne
As in when in your zone
Are you fully consumed
Are you fully in tune
It's a place where you're always
And never alone
Impossible to witness
Yet recognized
When occupied
Entirely to perfection
This selection of you
With the universe
Becomes true everything
It's nice device
When the you
Which is the one
That's having fun
Who usually remembers
Was just too busy being

WARPED SOCIETY

If our wheels
Are out of true
Then it may be
So very difficult
For you to be
True to you
With your senses
You sense what
Are your senseless
Or really seeing
From all I am
Seemingly fleeing
I am not freeing
What may be
Human in my being
From the realities
Of the now
Keep your kilter
Rolling smooth
Accepting the groove
Conditioned by
What do you choose
Begin in this moment
Actually experience
Fully and completely
Motivate, cultivate
Immediately strive
To see not
To be seen
And to let go
Of what is
In between
Our fantasies
Future and past
Nothing lasts
Not even then
Don't deflect
Direct perceptions

MRS. YOU

Breaking down
I cling to my frown
I recon I've been sinking
For a long while
A relentless creep
Has caught up to itself
Realizing I am fully steeped
Now oozing with denial
My smile has faded
In the midst of fetching
My now jaded inspection
No action parallels
My forged fulfillment
Too long I've created
The interim satisfaction of escape
It's all temporary anyways
But how long should one wait
For the tooth fairy
And does this leave
A valid debate
About hating...
Because you didn't see
That what was real
Was not your truth
How do you feel about this?
Who assumes they are complete?
Everything is proceeding
To set us up for defeat
I am now seeing
That my mind is mine
As is my heart
Yeah the one you stole
This of course was my course
In becoming more whole
I see clearly
Why you had to go
And in knowing what I missed
I miss you so

NIGHTY KNIGHT

Why it seems
That you are frightened
By all innocence
Pacing about
In this naked room
You assume the role
Of the Blind
Pulling yourself closed
You leave out
All sought experiences
But yet nil absorbed
As you stumble
From each to the next
Thinking that life itself
Indulged, will divulge
What hated purities
Are fading
In the sirens echo
As the distance between
You and the pillow
Is quickened

BELLS BELLS BELLS

A day like no other
Filled with laughter and love
Not that any day is ever the same
But today seemed to fit like a glove

Or maybe it was simply you
Everything felt so wonderfully pure
When there's love it will infect
And the remedy is to endure

Sometimes what is most obvious
Starring you right in the face
Like the feelings and connections one dreams about
Are suddenly there to embrace

And if it's not what you expected
That's even more so a symbol it's real
You know when things are effortless
Every moment somehow consciously surreal

You communicated through song
With your captivating golden sound
I looked deep beyond your eyes
And with gentle kisses I found

Something that felt so very wonderful
I hope you felt this too
You told me I could be the first to be the last
So perhaps this feeling isn't new

You see I clearly know how I feel about you
Our energy touched on a wholeness that is rare
But it was not something either was looking for
And now with the excitement I also feel scared

I value your friendship and person so much
Not to mention the obvious physical appeal

Cont.
And I know without thinking some things just make sense
Perhaps this you know even feeling half what I feel

But I have to be honest and don't want to play games
There are no coincidences along the way
I hope our connection continues to bloom
Thanks for sharing in such a magical day

TOTALLY

Differentiate this:
Do you antiquate bliss
In what states do you miss
Becoming whole
The universal goal
Goes far beyond
Whatever has come & gone
Learning that returning
To ourselves
Is happening now
It's how you perceive
What you believe
What will help
That will help
In the emergence
Of a unified Totality

INFECTIOUS

Love helps us create
There's no debate
And believing in fate
Is something that relates
To all possibility
While happiness sedated
Is for the jaded
My soul's is elated
To be in a place
That is pure
And I am sure
That beyond the allure
My friendships are a cure
For hardships endured
Moving on
We make choices,
Please have fun
Hear the voices
Pay attention, have respect
Did I mention Love infects?
Us all with what's good
And everybody should
Pass it on unconditionally
Should this not be traditionally
What is always passed on
We must confess and be real
What do you feel? Hearts you lift
What a wonderful gift
All my friends
You help mend
Any cracks in the soul
Feeling support
Helps make us whole
So necessary
This life can be, oh so scary
And when one is weary

Cont.
It's ok sometimes to be carried
Feeling sublime
Is impossible all the time
But through the divine
We can refine
While contentment is sought
You all ought to know
It's more so realized
Because of you
My Friends.
I hope you understand
What a big deal
You all are to me!

SETTING SAIL

So important when learning how to tie your own knot
That it's not tied to tight to shore
Cinch it snug around the love that you've got
Leaving some slack to explore
Yourself and each other, and what's in between
Pull up the spinnaker and float into your dream
Sometimes there'll be tension
And you might seem to get frayed
Survive the unknown together
That's how a joint future is made
With love all can be conquered
Far beyond the horizon unknown
Have faith that love will guide you there
With you the way I've already been shown

BEAUTIFUL YOU

Manifest Destiny
I confess to be
Yet somewhere in me
As much as I'm aware
I wonder if the things
Outside of myself
About which I so care
I can help along
Or perhaps that is wrong
Maybe defeating, personally misleading
For the big picture
Is this my script sir
Of course it is and my only cure
To confusion and doubt
Thinking life could go without
All of what I've had......
Is to let go
And only then do we grow
Re-balance and become
Still wanting to be one
With two under this sun
When your experiences suddenly make sense
And you've fallen off the good side of the fence
There's no need to look beyond
We are our own magic wands
What has been in front of you for some time
Is now so obvious the stars aligned
This is when your destiny is most clear
Yet I fear can be altered for the worse
If not patient, you will reveal this curse
What we have is what we already have
We must learn not to force or push
What is already beautiful!

PEDASTLED

Gracious in what you give
Inspired by how you live
Balanced, Refined, curious, you shine
Thanks for setting such an example
Of how one should live

MASKED FINISH

It's hard for me that we're apart
When I think how much we've done
When I ponder how much we've shared together
I wonder why we aren't still one
It doesn't seem right for it all to end
Can you really throw this all away
I think of you as my dearest friend
And I do so hope you'll stay
You once knew just how you felt
And now you are so unsure
I ask you what you feel for us
You say your feelings are just a blur
Before it was me who wore a mask
I pretended I was strong
Now I know exactly how I feel
And realize pretending is wrong
If only I hadn't been so stupid
Before we came to part
You might feel the same way now
As you did in the start

SUNDANCING

A lone deer
Caught in the peripheries
Stretches its legs
Bounding along as strong
As the steady train
In the open plains
Sounds a distinct whistle
It keeps its cadence
Matched if not
Almost attached
To the deer's attack
On the horizon
Close enough you can see
It kick up the dirt
Just far enough though
To wonder which way
Its ears stand alert
So prominent so dominant
In the open tundra
Of southern Bolivia's desert zones
Home to the Armadillo....
These Amerindians somehow
Could not just be left alone
And now in our global demise
It's prized to re group,
Re study, re boot
The ways of the wise
That have been relegated
Segregated, mitigated
Intimidated and degraded
For the purpose of a falsely created
Superfluous superior
Self proclaimed inferior
Ruling insidious
Overthrowing fear mongering
Self righteous
Backwards lifeless

Cont.

Fucks that suck
Everything from everything
And now want the words
To the song they have
Been trying so hard to sing
While ringing their own dinner bells
Inviting only themselves and whomever
Else delves in hell
Which society fell?
We'll wonder as this blunder
Ticks time in a backwards direction
Suddenly the selection
Of nature itself is evident
As what is lent by the significance
Of the lone deer.
I continue to peer out
The box cars open window
I see so far into the past
That the future evidently
Won't last without
The recollection of our infection
Being the trigger to selection
Of undoing what our ensuing
Unappeasable suddenly
Not very pleasing seething
Need for dominance
Has itself ourselves created
Understated indeed
Lets help the seed
Of this life rejuvenate
For all life's lives
Strive by concentrating
On the humanity
Of humanities issues

Cont.
That will return us
To our original stay
Still evident in today
Noticed on my way
In these vast lands of expanse
The prance of the deer
With its simplicity and synchronicity
Makes very clear
What we must manifest
To still work
As the train jerks and chugs on
The night befalls
And the darkness mimics
Our inflicted created
Who knows
Maybe fated
Ignorance
Let's not loose
The ways of necessity
Do you not want to dance freely
With the deer and the Armadillo
Esta TODO nessicito
Por Favor

NOTICE

So much hesitation
What do you wait on
People, others, brothers
Yourself
Tables….. For the work
With such little pay
Will you go berserk
What is enough
To wage your mind
I wonder about the choices
Creating such societal binds
Hanging on
You hesitate
Hanging out
You contemplate
Reliving your debates
Again and again
From change you refrain
What's your aim?
I wonder and ponder
Learning how to shoot straight
There's no debate in the weather
Man has a play in fate
Emancipate, you can
Without care of explanation
From those with the equation
That is before thought
About anyone else's situation
Anticipate ethically
It's not a personal dismissal
Everyone moves on

RISKY BUSINESS

He's your lover
Do you love him
Under the covers
What is getting played
Initializing satisfaction
Commitment less attraction
Convenient interaction
Will there come a day
That you grow into more
There is a risk of attachment
When intimacy is explored
I want to be your lover
I wonder if he loves her
I want to understand
Because somehow somewhere
You are still in my future plans

OLD PEEK

A lens through which I view
The evolution of differentiation
What combinations
Have been unlocked
And which sacridies
Have come to be mocked
We see progression
But what will be the lesson
Of our temperaments
In our tamporment
Of undermining
Our over mining
It is so very true
A lens through which I view
The beauty of you
Old mystical mountain
Named Matchu Picchu

LENDING RESOLVE

So many stresses
To solve, revolving
Around and about
Each and every day
But time and again
When I am in your presence
My stresses dissolve
And I just want to say
That this brilliance of solace
Is a perfect piece of mind
Where I seem always
To find peace
Praise you I do,
                    In kind

BACK POCKET LESSONS

Never let the beauty of resolve
Harden and get tucked away
Because then when you really need this exchange
You might subconsciously keep it at bay

And then there will be less good natured intent
Or desire to make things right
It's better to learn this lesson early in life
It never to late to let forgiveness take flight

So understand and try if you can
To always agree to disagree
Don't put up walls while mounting an offence
From different perspectives we must try to see

ALARM COCK

Follow through:
A prompt cue,
On time are you
With arrangements
That might do
Represent your egotistical
Mind frame
With the time game
Thinking yours
Is more important
While precluding yourself
Eluding the obvious
Didn't get the job
Prick job
Don't waste my time;
Touché

I LAUGH AT YOU

I have realized in time
That my happiness
Is mine, not yours
Happiness borrowed
Is a fictitious cure
Enduring sorrows
Has not much allure
But fantasy ensures
That tomorrow
Isn't as pure as now
Losing ones self
In projection
Is a misdirection
That skews
Non reality blues
Contentment
Can be misconstrued

Cont.
Through and through
And has nothing really
To do with you
Yeah I wish
I hear myself whisper
As I chuckle out loud

DON'T EVEN THINK ABOUT IT

Could awareness itself
Become an addiction
That creates contradiction
In that the affliction
Defeats being
Actually aware.
Too concerned
With the fare
Of attendance
That it becomes
A reduction
In perception
With an intuitive deflection
Of what is
Really happening.
Now is perfection,
Where lies
Your selection
Of attention
Which may be just
An invention
Of specific
Trains of thought

BUTTERED UP

A peanut buttered personality
Spread translucent thin
On the moldy crust
Of societies insatiability's
That you may see
In the tabloids
Holding void
Any truth, or any couth
Through the expedia
Of all media.
Who thought
You thought
Freedom of speech
Didn't mean
You'd be impeached
For points of view
That aren't even you
So many jam tarts
That interview
Stewing the misconstruing
Jumble of words
Into the absurd
No thanks honey
You can't even answer
Your own questions
Before you caress them

EXONERATION DATE

Forgiveness opens doors
And floors preconceptions
Of ideas that were more
Reflections of the beholder
Always colder
Through resentment.
With genuine contentment
There is no angst
Just subtle thanks
For the X perience
And clarity
On any delirium
That can cause disparity
Sometimes setting in
As soon as a relationship
Happens to begin
It's not whether you win
But yet are honest
While staying present
To exemplify and partake
While representing
What isn't fake
Because what's at stake
Is a reflection
Of your character
No need for the selection
Of processed blame
Causing an enduring pain
That is better forever
Released, this endeavor
Is easier said than done
I forgive myself,
For not forgiving you sooner

OBVIOUSLY

It's so wonderful
To have answers
To questions
That you didn't even have
I don't understand
She replied
The feeling you get,
When everything just makes sense
~ The glow emitting
From her contagious smile
Confirmed her understanding

SET UP

When the things that you dislike
Are related to with disdain
The doors of understanding swing shut
Sometimes it's best to refrain

From offering opinions
That are condescending in form
Causing unneeded friction
Leaving relationships torn

With love we can change
It helps so much to be heard
But as soon as we push
Our actions make meaningless our words

So what makes you angry
Can't be countered with the same
Unless we're actively compassionate
We'll be set up to feel unnecessary pain

TEMPTATION STATION

A privy of information
Could be a proxy
To the ultimate dissertation
No need though
To keep things in tow
That could create
Universal complications
And a lifetime
Of impure elations
Contributing to an inescapable
Personal probation
Perhaps a simple equation
But the power of temptation
Can haunt

SADDLE UP

To have an excess of hope
With no correlating action
Can inevitably bring about
Less than desired satisfaction

Things that are meant
To be or not to be
Can have certain factors leant
But in the end what I see

Is being bucked from the bull
And not getting back on
Thinking it's not in the cards
Suddenly you fold and are gone

Believe in your experiences
And learn from every one
Contribute to your hope
Dreams with effort will become

NIGHT TO QUEEN

As your tear trickles down
My fear of feeling is drown
Treading lightly
My frown is tickled
And I turn from a fickle
Adamant man
As quick as I can
Taking a flexible stand
Thinking what else
Could one expect
When checked?
Thanks mate

ALIGNMENT

The harvest moon
So Auratically full
The mystic and wonder
Enable us to dream
Good cheer turned from bad
The tables slowly turning
You face your designing ways
The confrontation is favorable
You absorb the cosmic radiance
You feel the being of being
The rain pours now, it is warm
Sometimes things couldn't go better
Other times not seemingly worse
Surrendering to your emotions
You are overwhelmed
Happiness brings tears
All overflowing with a smile
The stars align
There is a harvest moon

FORESHADOWED

How do you stack up
How's your luck buttercup
Under pressure
If you have to guess
Well you're certain I trust
At least that we must
Believe in the make
Of us humans as no mistake
All beings equal indeed
Since the first seed of invention
The dissension we've created
Has so many so jaded
I wonder often I do
If the characters behind
What are paraded
Looming in the uncalled
Shadows of whom
You're known to be
Is perhaps yet to be seen

CHOOSE YOUR WEAPON

We argue
But why
A confliction of words
I prefer to laugh and make peace
But instead we use swords
To stab and draw blood
Down it trickles each time
Again and again
You play with my mind
Each hole you create
Draws life from my soul
On purpose or not
They all take their toll
Bad habits have formed
That will scorn us all
If we keep living this fantasy
Soon we will fall
It doesn't make sense
To continue this charade
Delusions of happiness
They appear every day
To go on in such a way
Just doesn't seem right
We can follow our hearts
And learn not to fight
Peace is the answer
I think we must know
To the world and yourself
This is something we must show
So reach deep inside
Whoever we may be
Practice kindness and nurture
Set any negativity free

REMEDIATE

Divided
we fall
Destruct - shun
Not a con
Disasters
Going on
D fragmentation
D linquint see
D moral E
Speaking, with out diction
So many D's...
Does education
Become fiction
I am not seeking
A tried and true opinion
I've spied
And through dominion
I realize
That lies, all size
Are avenging on themselves
Strippers en vogue
Or maybe
Strippers thought rogues
Using a pole
Position
While they all keep wishing
To shower in gold
Oh what is sold
When blown for a buck
So Bre-ex I recon
Wasn't your luck?
It's all perpetual indeed
Not whole-istic
We ruin creed
And when done
All is bare and naked
Buy shunning morals

Cont.

We disgrace what's sacred
Peeling away purity
So much never to return
What's gone is no more
Selling our souls
Depleting to the core
Resource in our time
Is depleting exponentially
And I hope you all will find
It in yourself
To Dedicate all
To immeDiate change
It's time to
D side
D vise
&
D light
Before
D mise

CAUSE AND DEFLECT

Is fighting to have a cause
Better than fighting
For the cause
What is plausible
What cause will you try
To make peace for

PASSING LANE

Our narrow groove
That we tend to move
Through, does it what
Unless sooth
The half empty cup
That we most often choose
To guzzle from
We would better stand
Taller a man
With a muzzled insatiability
With our petty preoccupations
Sourcing out senile futility
In our unsighted "educated"
Interpretations of our needs
Resonating at a higher frequency
Blinding us to sounds and sights
That may come back to spite
In pass sings of joy
Not ever knowing
What freedoms we have missed
Blow your last kiss to me
And quench the parchment of man

LOW RIDER

Ups and downs
Smiles and frowns
Highs and lows
Ebbs and flows
Never always
Are we riding in style
Down this road
We may get lost for a while
If your pendulum has swung
In a negative regard
Then try to remember
Sometimes it's hard
To be happy when sad
And that's just fine
Try to accept
And not deflect
The Ying and the Yang

MIND MUSCLE

I so long to create
A life with you
My puzzled pieces
Are starting to fit
For so long I did await
While life just was
Still very busy
Creating me
More whole
The dog now wags the tail
Rather than
The tail wagging
The dog

SINKING HEARTS

Please describe to me
What I cannot see
Staring so hard
I make my plea….
It was so free,
Mutual and pure
I can't understand why
So much closeness
Doesn't endure
But doubt
Fills my head
Yet my heart
Has already been fed
The connection though,
It is slipping
Is that possible
It's not something
That I am gripping
To hard, am I?
From afar, I cry
Why push away
Why loose another day
Afraid of the past
Not to repeat, I pray
You pick me up
Don't let me down
We've barely started
Yet with a frown
I wonder if it's done
Yelling fuck you,
As loud as one can
Wondering what it takes
To be a noble man
I scream hanging on
Is my Independence gone
I'd rather share
This mystery

Cont.
Myself in you I see
Fuck you,
Individualization
Fuck you strength alone
Fuck temporary elation
Fuck sensationalized single homes
Fuck computer dating
Fuck not enough time
Fuck penciling in lunch
With someone else's
Indelible ink
I want to,
Fuck you….
What is forever really?
Who will endure?
What is necessity?
What is still pure
I want to need you
But I can't continue
What's in you
That makes my heart
So steadily sink

YES MASTER

Beat down, Kicked and broken
Mentally bruised my spirits croakin
I think I am fine yet I'm still soakin
In confusion and misery
A delusion that's no joke and
I try so hard to just let go
But it's not that easy and in order to grow
You must suffer through
With a half clear head
There is nothing else to do
That'll leave your soul fed
And hungry it remains
For answers and clarity
But it's hard not to pass blame
In the midst of disparity
Because of the love you gave away
And didn't reciprocated every day
The pieces, you pick them up
And may never truly understand
Yet it's very important to believe
It's all apart of the master plan

SHE CRIED

A craving for completeness
For a completer
Take a seat sir
This is a shock
An obsolete cure
I don't want to mock
But is that fake fur?
It's all an illusion
You were born pure
Where's the confusion
With yourself I'm sure
Already complete
But not yet absolute
I felt so much defeat
When my heart you cut loose
But I now have it back
Of that I am very certain
And the idea of a temporary
Solo performance
Has it's appeal
After the curtain
Was drawn so many times
I now find that
With our final act over
I was played in ways
That made me realize
You got the part
Of the competer
Not the completer
Bravo
She cried

ABSOLUTELY

For you in my heart
I had so much respect
Not displayed enough through action
Simply put was neglect

Never enough clarity
Until looking back
Which can be too late
I wish I then had the knack

To be more in control
Especially when on the fence
Acting at times with ill logic
To me makes little sense

And when you're in love
You must have patience throughout
Don't torch up your bridges
With the ol'scream and shout

I do know this behavior
Will quickly tarnish the soul
Chiseling down what you stand for
Slowly becoming less whole

We must act with integrity
Cherish with behavior that you adore
If this is not your absolute
Then what you love will be no more

TRANSIT

With launch codes proper
Holding patterns complete
What might you meet
On the other side of take off
With a disgruntled cough
I get me own attention
Taken back, I wonder
Who lacks space
In their overhead compartments
Weightless the tarmac disappears
Into societies bustle
Corralled in different gates
Awaiting for the time to soar
Some early, some late
Controlled by the cadence
Of outstretched strides
Following through
Some following you
It's like a Nascar race
With a jet fueled pace
I brace for the escalator
Giving welcome
To an often assisted space
That gets you accustomed
While anticipating escalation
Is it reasonable to be prepared
For some minor body damage
Landing is definitely grounding
But usually the scariest part

HEAD BAND AID

Compulsive, incessant
A dilemma, unpleasant
To wrap your head
Around thought
Without awareness
One gets caught
Up with fallacy
Non reality
Perhaps becoming free
Means wrapping thoughts
Around your head
Synched tight
For the right
Thinking to absorb
Recording of course
Our depth
As everything

OH DADDY-O

Everything in moderation I preached was key
Turning cheek to persistent debauchery
All accepted in our warped society
Not having in line any personal priority
Unfortunately allowed do to other responsibility
Surprisingly adding up to as ten year spree
Turning into my father could I be?
Not motivated to accomplish is what I see
Trapped in a bottle, never free
A pile up of hurt and mental debris
Stemming from a broken family tree
A moral direction with action takes bravery
Changing one's ways with discipline and integrity
Repetition of the same leaves who you'll always be

THERE YOU ARE

Your poetic grace
Helps erase
Anything but pure thought
The infinity understood
In our affinity
Mightily sublime
Your pure lines
Banish all time
Plucked from the heavens
You blanket all
With pre-established harmony
A mystical connection
An incurable infection
Of passion and enchantment
Every day.....jah vu
Explains the quantum you
With surging emotion
I see seemingly deeper
Than every and all possibility
Our inner unity
I feel
Will succeed
In lending resolve
To all difficulties
In truth
We are
Our everything

GOT A SECOND

To be in your time
You may or may not
Be on time
And in time itself
Time and time again
We'll be out
As time ticks in
Sometimes ticking off
Always ticking on.
Just a minute please
At ease, we see
That timing is all
All is timing
Time just is
What…another time out
Is everything hours
Or is the timing
That is everything
Ours
Be of your time
This time is yours
I thought
Your time is
Our time
Be off
This time
It's on
You're timed
Go;
Aloha Mr. hand

CULTIVATION

Without acceptance
Anguish would conquer
Overcome our beings,
Break and shard our souls
Pride yourself with change
Create positivity,
Open your arms
Realize
L O V E
Cultivate an embrace
Of yourself
With others
From our roots we are driven
By pulse, beats, and rhythm
Allow a positive flow
Low or high,
Always frequent
Sea to sky......
And beyond

PIXY DUST

Fairy tales
Of we
I see in the sea
Of your gauzy wings
Glistening with
All you dew
Your radiance
Penetrates into
Forever......
With a soothing calm
My gleaming soul
Is uncontainable
Bursting with pride
To collide, I confide
With you
It was fusion
Your magic passed on
From being
It's no illusion
I cherish our connection
Perspective is perfection
Without thought
My affection overwhelms
Thank you perfect pixy

I BELIEVE that we will better ourselves as individuals if every day we put ourselves in an uncomfortable, better put; challenging, perhaps fearful (personally), or awkward situation, and overcome it with patience and sought after understanding, essentially becoming the feelings that are evoked, learning from this in a way that through inner strength, gentleness, and respect, you allow yourself a clarity that helps you get closer to potential, in turn, becoming more in tune, and more complete.

In contrast to feeling more complete, having been challenged by love I feel less whole than imaginable.

Some things in Life, very few, but a few all the same, just make sense. They make sense with what we've learned, what we want to learn, who we want to be (knowing it or not), who we are, what we know and don't know, and most importantly what and how we feel. When the unimaginable happens, and the stars align for what would be less than even a mere moment, if you are in tune, forever after one is changed and will never fail to remember.

When something obvious yet beyond description, beyond definition, beyond imagination, I guess yes, beyond words, when this is questioned, fraudulent or defiled, rational understanding can become temporarily disabled.

We must nurture and nourish, in order to flourish, never take for granted, have reserved kindness an love. Can we not show emotion without judgment? No two the same, but we try in this game, to convince of what's right, see the light, is there really a need to fight, in the dark we're alone, when needed most why isn't love shown, you are you, an individual, different yet the same, why cause this pain, it's not a game, we've already won because we're one, like the shining sun, we allow reason to live, to laugh, to cry, and to learn, to grow and to cherish, ourselves and each other, all, along this way.

When we fail to realize what the consequence of acting in haste, with haste, through haste, will be, inevitably we may lose the ability to behave with gentleness and compassion, with reason and wisdom, and with enthusiasm. Overriding your instinct and emotion at times is an essential quality, mandatory even in contrast to our own subconscious and even our conscious instinctive views and perspectives.

In love we must accept and realize that it is the differences and uniqueness of each individual that make the relationship one of a kind.

I DO

Love as a feeling
So appealing
When received
I believe
That possibility
Beyond self
Is conceived
When the support
From another
Is unconditional
It's like no other
Feeling in the world
Not unlike the boy or girl
Who know love
I hope, from family
I see what can be
From falling in love
Can bring very different
Potential and possibility
Beyond what individually
Could be understood.....
First One,
        before the other.

REUBIN SANGER

Dare to dream
Realize potential
Perseverance and will
Will overcome

Obstacles of societal norms
Conditioned to believe
So many people blowing their own horns
Are we that fucking naive

The insecurity of religion
Judgment addiction and greed
Expected to deliver like a carrier pigeon
Will our minds ever truly be freed?

Pee Wee's elation
The MASTERBATION Equation
Lead to a certain DEGREDATION
And INSTITUTIONALIZATION
What REALIZATION
May cum from this

Look into your eyes
A mirror of the soul
Can you see any lies
Do you feel whole?

We must calm our angst
And heal our wounds
Come to terms with our existence
And if ever taking anything for granted
Straight up beat it

MYSTIC OPTIMISTIC

Do we dare challenge accepted assumptions
What do you perceive to be true
Will you choose a path of voiced opinions
Or hold your breath until you turn blue

Sequential repetitions
Of feet that hit the ground
Throughout this precious onward march
We must stay real in our frowns

They may only last a moment
Always optimistic of what's ahead
Dare to journey the unknown path
Allow your curiosity to be fed

The possibilities of everything are endless
This can cause hysteria in the mind
The more you know the less you know
Easily lost in the midst I find

Stimulate and provoke thought
Take the time to learn
Speak your mind with clarity
Let enlightenment take its turn

INFATUATION

I didn't realize how dissatisfying it is
To have a lost lover
That is still in your life
You can't choose the time
That you'll be able to fully let go
But it's necessary to rid yourself of contention
That false hope created far after it was done
It's natural to want to hang on
To a person that helped you envision forever
And that in ways you've think you've become
But without this misunderstood understanding
You wouldn't see eternity again
And when you realize this person is not you
It's easier to release any unnecessary pain?
You definitely had a part in the chase
Nothing can be erased
So accept and move on
Or don't accept, that's not wrong
But move forward
From what is gone
With lessons presented
In every dawn
There were so many chances
Time and time again
Not enough slow dances
Why is it so hard to start out as friends
First prove you to you
Most satisfying in any end
Change you're not done until you re through
Always takes some time to mend
It's hard to allow what is
Without experience
But knowing who you don't want to be
Will help you love on

DECISIONS DECISIONS

The choices we make
Over and again
Putting us through turmoil
Can create a superfluous of pain

And they are choices at the time
Even looking back into the past
That seem for once could end fine
The downward spiral couldn't last

The old one toke backstroke
Has me swimming circles for sure
In this vortex I've been lucky
While trying to endure

So much has gone wrong,
In turn much went right
I see making better choices
Will leave nothing to spite

Paying everything really
But the ultimate price
While being given more chances
Than is comprehensible in one life

Is tough when you think you're figured
And apparently thought out
Foolishly after the fact again
Leaves more adversity no doubt

But in the mean time you rejuvenate
Feeling some sought after growth
Everything seems so clear sometimes
You know what you loath

Cont.

Oh all the decisions that you've made before
Yes the ones that never saw any action
Even though you believed in yourself to the core
You had no follow through leaving no satisfaction

You'd make commitments cognitively
Decisions that were never hard to make
With such powerful thought out precision
Your claim you were going to finally steak

But the rotisserie you spin
Has your backbone on fire
Strength isn't that strong
Until it's applied with desire

And when strength is called upon
That's the moment of truth
It's easy to step back in
To what temporarily sooths

So to actually see change
Not just understand what is strength
Will take a solid rearrange
You need to know to what lengths

You're prepared to commit
Because the back strokes of time
Will wait for no one at all
There is no rewind

Singing the same song
Over and over again
Will mean that when figuring this out
That your potential my friend

Cont.

May have been wasted away
You figured you were in control
But when you needed to be strongest
You seemed to routinely let go

And be rights still to this day
The choices most often were
Made while thinking you had standards
Which now seem somewhat obscure

Thinking all the time
Control was easy and would be shown
It was your option to draw the line
Yet so many times this option was blown

It's all so clear in retrospect
Convincing me hasn't been that hard
But not getting beyond the starting gate
Truth be told isn't getting me very far

MIRROR MIRROR

If you are a reflection
Of an illusion
Then you are loosing
The perfection
By choosing
A x-section
Of what is real
The mirror on the wall
Said back to me

APPETITE FOR DESTRUCTION

My Cravings are diminishing for an uncontrolled existence
Riding myself of the confusion I bring,
By never personally attempting resistance
Against the direction the pendulum swings

When you represent certain trains of thought
That lead you to simple escapes
They can cause a slow, drawn out mental rot
Throughout time this has left little debate

Commitment and inspiration are what one needs
Insatiable by nature we can be easily misled
It takes some practice to be present and strong
Keep this info the back of your head

At times it may seem counterintuitive
And consuming beyond any conviction
To explore potential in every regard
But you couldn't really have a better addiction

EMBRACE

One second per second
And on we will go
Always becoming this time
Never fast nor slow

Two seconds I recon
In this time you grow
Are you waiting in line
To get into your show?

Our perfection of pace
Sped up, slowed down
Relative to the clock
Whose hands are bound?

Sometimes more time
Can be easily a waste
Should we then fall behind
In this lifelong race

We'll have more time to catch up
We don't need to chase
Always fast for show
Slow down and embrace

ASSOCIATION

Formless
Form
Dimensions
We're born
Exploitation
Sexuality
Pornographic
Scorn
Mentality
Between
Intentions
Life
Manuals
Inventions
Disease
Strife
Intellect
Compassion
Poison
Seas
Definition
Labels
Medias
Breeze
Crime
Poverty
Imbalance
Thirsty
Infection
Time
Wisdom
Bursting
Refine
Maps
Plans
Implementation

Cont.
Logging
Flowers
Robots
Masturbation
Health
Cancer
Drought
Gasoline
Oxygen
Bars
Doubt
Neoprene
Chocolate
Factories
Clones
Continents
Bombs
Fruit
Medicine
Wanting hints
Peyote
Horses
Loot
Masters
Jokers
Battery
Charging
Disasters
Credit
Crutches
Sugar
Coke
Marge
OJ
Scurvy
Tokes
Cartoons

Cont.
Computers
Poverty
War
Pollution
Shooters
Vegas
Poor
Gaps
Dessert
Pie
Math
Infinity
Cars
Surprise
Bath
Why
Letters
Sounds
History
Channel
Beatles
Bugs
Mystery
Explosions
Presidents
Flannel
Seasons
Blender
Speed
Breaks
Treason
Purity
Love
Takes
Action
Everything's

Cont.
Fleeting
Satisfaction
Is meeting you
All Arrangements
Have been made

WET FEET

A saturated infatuation
Dueling the banjos
Of emotion and logic
Snapping heartstrings
From rockin out in that hard place
We all erase
Memories of fret
While creating more
What's in store?
Feet again wet
The inevitable is….!
Vulnerability
Building on experience
Harmonization; elation
Manifestation of a migration
Through action and sensation
Creation is love
Your caramelized curves
Are the catalyst for my fantasies
Even in my dreams
You still leave me breathless
In contrast to life's resonating imperfections
Pick your becoming
While strumming your song
Our celestial rhythm is one

RE-PROJECTION

When you are somewhere else
While daydreaming beyond
What is then, the present moment
Most likely already gone
We spend an immensity of time
Immersed in the surreal
Projecting our whereabouts
To a place with more appeal?
What is really more appealing
Than where you are, which is right here
Is it ever clear why you are stealing
Your reflection from the mirror
Of your dissections and projections
Within the perfection of the continuum
Residing inside your fantasies
When will you make the connection
Between these moments and reality
What can be?
Already is

O.P.C.

If you can remove the things that matter to other people in terms of who they think you should/could be, then underlying will be what really matters to you. Then, essentially, all there will be to live up to and respect will be first and foremost yourself. This of course minding manners tact and couth.
We all weigh very heavily on what other people think that in a sense we condition ourselves to be conditioned by other peoples conditions.

VOLUNTEERED CHANGE

Oscillation of thought
Reacting in time
Phantom manifestation
Might, ..will
Dissect the minded mind
Can we connect emotion
To the physical fortress
While the mental
Liberation reflects
Do All understand sensation
We definitely crave elation
Don't miss the facts
Theories to be exact
Probation can defeat
And what's accomplished
Can and will conceit
We tend to repeat
With a lackadaisical
Concentration
But the drawbridge
Like the bow
Is drawn with grace?
Sometimes our intentions show
That we cut out
To feel strong
Cupids arrows though
Do belong
Necessitations
Of both sides
Penetrate, Coincide
Why erase the future
Before it can unfold
Equally, do you see
That we need more
This wanting is a chore
The same spiel
The same helm

Cont.

Different vessel
Different realm
Different pace
Same destination
Live with grace
In this great creation
There are no winners
If we disgrace
Volunteer inner stillness
Undress Ego
From it's fallacy
Of needing to be….
Oh so strong
Be slow, emote the now
Be hear but not
UN attending
To the prowess that can jade
Vulnerability keeps one real
We be damned
And try to steal
The hearts of queens
Only lend truth
Give freely
But still defend
Wisdom and humanity
Through time
We can gain sanity
Let go
Go on ……show
Growth
Look in
Shout out
And be
Still
Understanding
That hanging on
For more hanging out

Cont.
Is what
What is?
Everything
When?
All is gone
As it happens
Ahead is impossible
In the now
Defend integrity
While learning
To regress
Create strength
Through simplicity
Don't let
The understood complications
Complicate

This revision was lengthened and changed extensively with an
    undecided result.

The next poem is the original:

Oscillation of thought
Reacting in time
Phantom manifestation
Dissecting the mind
Connecting emotion
To the physical fortress
While mental liberation
Reflects all sensation
Controlling the drawbridge
To a vaster realm
Volunteer inner stillness
Undress ego
From its fallacy of armor
Emote the now

SYNOPSE / SYNAPSE

After reading them again and making a few more changes, I think I
finally like them both and dig how one thing can flow into another
and still have distinctly different feelings.
I have tried, maybe not hard enough, but am getting better, towards
getting things out and on paper when the thoughts first arise or
appear. Often I will have what I think is a great inspiring insight or
intrigue that I could see turning into poetry but let the moment pass
being completely convinced that I will remember it later. Seldom to
never do I. So when transferring the above and feeling a different
direction I just let it go and realized that that is catalyst to the creative
process. Timing and action, on, and in the moment when the bulb
lights up. Writing can be very subjective. I suggest writing when you
are inspired or intrigued, it can manifest surprising results...

PORT WHOLE

By theory, if you dig deep enough, with grave effort, no pun intended,
buy the time, I mean by the time, you exhaust your present vessel,
your path will end and start at a portal to the nucleus of ultimate and
eternal rejuvenation…
NO?

JEOPARDY

I'd like to buy another owl Valex
I'll take Another E
I believe I'll solve the puzzle
The question is:
What letter is at the start of the Canadian alphabet?
That would be obviously be an EH

WHO'S IN CHARGE HERE

Lacadazia maniacal
A stack of pages will
Try to be filled
By your pen.....
Initially blank
Will you defend
Your proverbial rank
As a superior being
Never fleeing
In times of tribulation
The lawns of our yard
Will continue
Through gestation
To grow and to grow
On both sides of the fence
Creating a destiny
That from beginning to end
Lends all to adaptation

Cont.

Situated in your irrigation
With innate ability and desire
To tend to its necessity
Complimentary, like the honey bee
Pollinating the flower
Yet thinking mindlessly
That it may be in power
What allowance do you give
To the possibility
Of everything alive
Living beyond our intellect
Collects ability to be
Ultimately free
Through unity and adaptation
Of changing by not really changing
Some things really do just work
But our human quirks
Are tampering with
The everything
Of a simply observant harmony

HELLO THERE

Waking up
To who you've created
Yes, what you over time have become
Suddenly it seems you're not very elated
About a life to which you've succumb
Fun it's been along the way
But the easy road, was easy to take
You seem to be losing confidence every day
Once your confidence was hard to shake
Now being rattled with confusion at large
This seems a good point to really dive in
There is still time for you to take charge
Now is when you need to begin
Re-inventing I see can create insecurities
For the first time, you may feel regret
It's due time to get back to life's purities
In to yourself you need to check

ABSINTH IN MIND

Maybe the ones
Gone first
Are closer
To forever
Maybe the absinth
In mind
Could bring us closer
To what is never
A dimension
That is severed
From dementia
That would be clever
If we ever
Sorted out
The proper route
~Whatever.......
The case may be
Right here, I hear right
Because what's left
Is despite
The fight, or flight
There are never, mmm ....any content
Where have all the messengers been sent?

Originally, what was written, before a very quick re-write/re-read, where new ideas always seem to rapidly spawn, but also, sometimes, inevitably take away from the original insight or inspiration, is below these notes.

It's a fine line to a completely different poem, when indeed some finals are as finished as the second the ink hits the page, and can no matter what other thoughts flow and arise when goings over, be any better for what they were or even weren't meant to be. This is creative intuitively unleashed in a pure state.

These two versions I am uncertain about in how the examples of what's tried to be described above, (not in the poems themselves), accurately explain the process, but all the same I hope there is some understanding in my explanation of triggered thought beyond the intention, if at all there can be specific intention beyond the beginning without it changing constantly. I think possible with any first writing but not so much with a second. I also think if it can be worked again than it should be to a point, it's not finished until it is complete which would not allow, from the writers view anyways, any better script.

Original:

ABSENCE OF MIND

maybe the ones gone first
are closer to forever
maybe the absence of mind
could bring us closer to never
whatever the case may be
here there's never many content
the planet may be gone already
the first messengers have been sent

S.V. ANSCOMBE

The mountains stretch upwards
In a sleepy yawn
While the precursor of dawn
Fore lays a calm perspective
That is extraordinarily magnificent
All is glistening refraction
The totality of satisfaction
Is reflected as I glance yonder
Pondering finally nothing
Head slowly turning
My peripheral yearning
For the perfect circle
In this once perfect circle of life
It helps not to compete
When in search of anything complete
These thoughts are fleeting
As I re-absorb this moment
Worries are whispered away
As the whitecaps slowly stray
In a gentle exhale
Of a unified breath
Their quest is at best
Repetitive liquidity
I see them reform
And dissolve and re-form
And evolve again reborn
In a splendid morning
On the pristine waters
Of Kootenay Lake

MIND MAKE UP

A deprivation of humanity
With your judgmental equation
Not allowing thee
To exist ever naturally
The pre-packaging
That you represent
Has consequence
Because however easy sleazy
Your points of view
Are swallowed they are hollow
Pertaining more so to you
Mr. magoo.
We need create
While curbing
Our initial innate
Points on queue
Of who and how we view
Through only our own eyes.
Thank you but I despise
Being swayed until first hand
I can see you portray
Yourself

MIND MATTERS

My patience for ignorance
Sometimes wears very thin
It snaps with great tension
An invasion within
Control overtaken
All of which I loose
I am not faking
In fact I am shaking
When madness overwhelms
My brain
My brain
It hurts
But there's no pain
Sustain, refrain, regain
Or go insane
What the fuck is this game
Different opinions
Not right or wrong or left behind
Center, yourself
EVERYWHERE
EVERYTHING
All going on
Atomic Silence,
Paralyzed, perplexed
Eternal sadness
Endless raddness
My mind, do you mind, someone's mind
Mind your mind
If you can
Moving, Still…lacking control
Feelings of chaos
Overriding logic
It's not hard to do
For me for you
Everything you know
Is nothing

Cont.
Nothing matters
It shouldn't matter
We are matter
I, OH YOU, WE, US
All entities of our own
All matter
Insanity for a second
Normalcy for less
Who decides
WE think we know
WE know we think
Who fucking knows?
Sometimes it's best not to…..

BYE BYE

Anxious about what you want to get done
Takes away from enjoying what's already in place
It's great to have objectives, new visions and goals
Yet slowing down can help you absorb your own pace
It's impossible for everything to happen all at once
Except this is in fact what is actually going on
Enjoying the process of this challenging life
Because the end result…….
Well it's inevitably gone

THE GOOD'OL DAYS

We're living in a time
That our last human connection
To when there was simplicity
Will soon only be a reflection

That is documented in words,
Early voice recordings and photographs
That were magically captured by technology
On vinyl and pinhole cameras from the past

When my grandparents were kids
There were no plains or computers
No cell phones or space ships
No suburbs or commuters

No wholes in the ozone
No past peak productions
They played hockey on ponds
There were no Ikea instructions

Ponder their views,
Certainly ones of confusion
About this crazed society
That no doubt is loosing

Touch with real values
While we blindly keep cruising
Not to long till the rides over
What kind of fait are we choosing?

With this techno illogical absurd direction
In actuality humanity seems a massive infection
That is whittling any potential for our protection
And the sad thing it's our own elections

Were passing the point of no return
Passing the joint don't get burned

Cont.

What do you think it is we will have learned?
When there's not another dollar to be earned

It's so consuming to be born insatiable
But the snowball is still gaining speed
I think that if it picks up any more paces we will
Slip as it melts into the heat of hunger and greed

Please create some time to sit and listen
To stories that can still first hand be told
About the things that will soon be missing
As another generation unfolds and grows old

We need to regress to progress I recon
We've set ourselves up for quite the blunder
I think what we need is something Willy Wonka said best
A revolutionary non-pollution mechanical wonder

It's hard to put in context our grandparents as kids
It definitely wasn't such a long time ago
Imagining this time when values weren't $ signs
When people lived more for necessity than show

That is a time to which were still directly connected
A time when affording to be alive
Wasn't classified as a world pandemic
Imagine the struggle for our kids, kids to survive

It's hard to convince or have sink in
To the people who have survival on their minds
That they need to recycle and help fix global warming
When it's food for their family they're trying to find

Cont.

I know the poor have less part in polluting
But I hope that you do understand
That the problems we're facing are exponential
And they must involve everyone as a part of the plan

That needs to be implemented yesterday for certain
If we all paid attention just a wee bit more
To how our grandparents' generation grew up
We wouldn't have to be as frightened about what's in store

That inevitably will demolish the populations' possibilities
Of even being grandparents at all
What ever happened to the good old days?
When you could put coins in pay phones;
                    I think it's time that we make the call

CLOAKING DEVICE

Do you practice what you preach
Or suit yourself just for the day
Do you maybe practice preaching
Or are you blind to your ways

Do you find refuge a personal breach
That you yourself betray
Beyond yourself are you reaching
To keep the truth at bay

Who is it we expect to teach
When with our heads you tend to play
To whose ideals are we leaching
Can't we coincide with what we want to portray

CAT WALK

Conceptual models
Separated form there bottles
Molded, created
Coincided, segregated
Paraded, exploited
Becoming jaded
Who really enjoyed it
Runways, airplanes
Some day's cocaine
Why refrain
You'll pass the blame
Anyways
The fast tracked days
Of Fabrications
And false sensations
Where is the emancipation
When hiding under the covers
Of magazines
Those air brushed scenes
Still have you eating less
Than rice and beans
Wafer thin
Like your saltines
On 10 grand
Each hour
What an influence
Of superficial power
This makes so sour
The people really
Starving in this world

YOU RULE

No one's fooling
Who's ruling
Why are we dueling
With temptation
When the equation
Adds a false elation
We are meant to govern
Via the power of choice
What voice is being heard

Or in a simpler form:

Some lives are ruled by temptation
When they could be governed by the power of choice

THE END

Make nothing new
There's already too much
Why the crutch
Of consumption
Consuming
I am not assuming
It's a problem
And I am fuming
Of exhaustion
The man will fold
His hand was sold
With everything
What position
Do you hold?
No couth…
A duvet on the truth
Keeping it warm
Yet what's uncovered
Is as cold as can be
Nobodies free
From what's is unfolding
The loading
Of immensity
Beyond defense
The shopping spree
For domination
Defies creation
And what has spawned
An obvious time ago
So slow, to fast
We assume
Things will last
While grooming
The opposite
Of what is looming
Now we can watch

Cont.
The undoing
Of everything
Ensuing......
            the end

EL TORO

It's easy to paint a bright future
When you're flying on leaners and brew
But the energy already borrowed from tomorrow
Leaves the next day with nothing seen through

And time will inevitably catch up with itself
Still cheerful prospects around the next bend
But wasted health, ability and consciousness
Will speed up your trip in the end

Except in the midst of the process
It may seem slower than one can conceive
When every day after is like the one lived before
Why can't we commit to whom and what we believe

CONVINCING ABILITY

Everyone is looking for an alternate route
Altering sense and fear
Drowning the models
Of societies white picket fences
What is it that you hold so dear
Why are we frayed, please stay,
For today?
Be true for a significant time
Never again go thrashing around
Pretending that all is just fine
What is time......
If it's not taken
Certainly a crime if I'm not mistaken
There's no faking when you commit
And that's just it
To stay clear, can bring fear
We rarely steer away from temptation
Then the contemplation
Of every changing situation
Confuses progress
Yet on it all goes
No matter your part from the start
This happens until it all stops
And I give props to the folk
Who don't take life as a joke
Who learn and laugh and cry and grow
Fast or slow, they nurture and give
Listen and live, strained through life's siv
They take on global pain
Trying to stay sane, yet losing themselves
In their intangibles
The heart and the soul
And your spirit when you're whole
Allows a connection with thoughtlessness
Everything makes sense in Love......
But aren't we all in love with our ability ....
        To convince ourselves of anything?

FLASHES THROUGH TIME

Suddenly you remember something
That before you didn't know
Perhaps allowing a simple insight
Into happenings lifetimes ago
Or maybe it's a different dimension
That has a most similar flow
All to help the process of becoming
Which tends to happen so very slow
Yes this may be somewhat confusing
Because all of these flashes in time
Seemingly happen so quickly
Then they're suddenly gone from the mind
Leaving always a subtle part of an imprint
To our magical celestial design
That we instinctively try to piece together
In order to simply refine
There's no question we must do this personally
But more imperatively globally as well
It would seem not a complicated concept
Yet near impossible to have everything gel
So pay grave attention to the little glitches
That paradoxically do and don't make much sense
We have less than little time to be wasting
While teetering on both sides of the fence
I can't believe that compared to intellect
All else could be considered less dense
If we fail to learn from the past and present, right now
I fear the future will hold no brilliance

FORCE FEED

A step back in time
Why should we rewind
Unless it's used to move foreword
And untangle the mind.
Can the freedom of choice
Be taken away
Can the freedom of thought
Create an array
Of different directions
An individual course
Who's really empowered
Who feels the remorse
Is it the people who govern
Triple standards at least
They bring our food to their tables
Toasting another great feast
Take away opportunity
And some are forced to conform
With no other options
History is somehow reborn
Look through the smoke and mirrors
In order, to stay sane
Remember some doors have to shut
Before they can open again.

REPRESENT

A machine gun sentence
Shot from the hip
Heavy on the trigger
You unload your clip

And you realize your words
As they pierce through the soul
Leave you lacking any dignity
Now who is less the whole?

Think for a moment please
Or maybe even two
About how you represent yourself
We all need to think things through

So many people react
In such inexcusable ways
With no control over our instinct
We can't keep impulses at bay

So try to be the noble person
Cherish letting some things go
Sometimes we need not prove our point
Who is the person you want to show

QUANTIFIED

It's the theory of chaos
That's chaotic in itself
Because the mind will never grasp
What exactly has been dealt

It will simply remain always unknown
Which is actually a straightforward point
Creating a chaos entirely its own
Like being completely ripped on a joint…..

……understanding of the space were in
We tend to constantly overload the mind
With all the possibilities of how and when did this begin
Yet how can't we ponder the boundaries of our time

And space, and left versus what's right
With everything apart of the whole
A butterfly takes flight at the tip of the south
And a typhoon takes out the north pole

The relativity can be based on what ifs
So impossible to ever really know
But in understanding this life is a gift
With time your wisdom can let chaos go

ANSWER BOUND

Sometimes I feel trapped in my head
And my feelings just stepped outside
The rest of me, even what I don't think
Seems to be trying to hide

Scared of who I'm not
Of who I want to be
Scared of where I'm going
Of what I will, and will not see

Inevitably life is a paradox
We are born and begin to die
In the end we'll learn how little we know
I can't help but ask the question why

Wanting to know the all of everything
Creates irriticity in my mind
Not knowing how or which foot to put forth
Can certainly cause a futile bind

PRECIOUS WASTE

Is everything really ever
Simply as it seems
How far past our truths
Does reality lean
To the write or the left
They're just words we speak
Communication though is key
Yet there's so much tongue in cheek
Be who you are, that's not me
Our hearts must stay open
Do we just let people be?
Live to the fullest
Express how you feel
Try to always be kind
And always be real
Try not to draw lines
Between color or race
Human life is too precious
To let go to waste
You are here for this time
In which we have been allowed
So remember that life
Is not just if you live,
But also how

HYPOCRO CITY

Sometimes everything seems so unreal
Literally; I don't know how I should feel
It all seems fucked up beyond repair
Yet who are we to think things aren't fair

Is anything worth trying to really figure out?
Is it fair to yourself to have so much doubt
Doubt about everything including who you are
Take the time out to wish upon the stars

Beyond what we know it's a constant race
These are exactly the problems that we continue to face
And the trusted, so convincing, that's what they know best
Accepted theories become fact, can't we just let them rest

Apparently not, it's instinctive to want more
It's nature to be curious, to open that door
But don't be surprised if it's an unknown sight
That leads to an eternal, no holds bar fight

About the possibility of everything, of what could be
Don't get too caught up, try to set yourself free
We all want the right answers, you make the call
You've been empowered with choice, use it don't stall

It all sounds so easy but actions are louder than words
So this struggle with hypocrisy seems more than absurd
Take responsibility for your life, present, future, and past
Try not to have regrets, it all happens to fast

DIABLO

Expecting the extended party
You have definitely put in your time
Except this is exactly the downfall
That comes from the light of the lime

Never compensating in a valued manor
But you get by so it's never your fault
Yet only perfect practice makes perfect they say
Do things really taste better with salt?

Or are we only masking the flavor
Of the things in which we needn't any more
So we can convince ourselves things aren't as they seem
With the bottled up help of ol'El'himador

OH BROTHER OH MOTHER

WE must analyze and realize
Look with our eyes
Help re-route our certain demise
Hear the cries
Of our ignorance
Before she dies
We must devise
A plan with size
So we can all survive
And have the opportunity
To Experience love
Why let Chaos, Destruction, and Fear Rule

SAVING ACCOUNT ABILITY

The predicament of change
A certain fear to re-arrange
We crave hiatus from our minds
In a world we may never find
An endless search for just a little bit more
In quest for yourself
Through someone else's open door
Trying to escape,
What lies at the core?
An elusive mystery....
Letting go is a chore
Adaptability is change,
Revealed in many forms
Can't we acquire enough sense
To survive societal norms?
But what kind of sense
Is it that we all crave
How much is enough
Can yourself you still save?

I HOPE SO

;
~~HAVE HOPE NOT EXPECTATIONS~~
~~ALTHOUGH THEY'RE MORE OR LESS THE SAME~~
~~WHEN CHANGE IS THE ONLY CONSTANT~~
~~ONE WILL SURELY CAUSE LESS PAIN~~

HERE YOU ARE

A missed- intentioned
Awakened dimension
Brings spiritual revival
Necessary for survival
A validation of existence
In beyond what is here
Is a place seldom ventured
Because of an unspoken fear
That is conditioned in most
Oh the comforts that bind
With the securities and routines
That are learned throughout time
Don't allow letting go
Create a false sense of what's real
Try to preserve what's left pure
For there's no time we can steal....
When you feel the aforementioned
Have intention preconceived
And believe
You have not missed a thing
Here you are

OH REALLY

Are we paralled to our parallels
In a universe
That has a paradigmed
Human curse
Paralleling its parallels.
Are we not versed to tell?
How dare we sell
Out on this idea
It may free ya
When you look back
Through your own black holes

TIME FRAMES TIME

People can grow up
@ only their personal speed
And when it happens all of a sudden
You may feel magically freed
But it will take continued commitment
To see what you have learned through
Integrating your mind and action
Tends to be a hard thing to do
Because when you are confident in your ability
And you know who you can be
It's never a question of if you can change
But then you don't and this I see
As something that is personally fraudulent
Becoming undeniably a fallacy
It certainly wasn't what you really meant
To have happen, who do you want to be

SHREDDING DEEP POW

Your picturesque Virtuoso
You languishing liquid eyes
Let me float away
In your visions
Of our future
With your rounded forms
Grace is forever re-born
You are an expression
Of everything precious
Exceeding understood beauty

EXHALE

I am devoured by the warmth
The water overcomes me
It becomes me ⁓
      As I breathe
I observe, my chest submerges
Filling with life, again it rises
Recycling this cycle
That is needed and repeated ⁓
      And I breathe
I am in a rhythm
My pulse ever present
Not the beating of my heart ⁓
      Because I breathe
But the connection with existence
Everything's allowed
This regularity of vibration
All happening at different frequencies ⁓
Relaxed I yawn and get out of the bath

SHAPING FORM

Can we continue to re form
While holding on to what is
Our shape?
When out of shape
Have we lost our structure
Or do we continuously
Prolong being
While being re-born
In the shape of
Our other forms?

DIFFERENT BUT THE SAME

To wonder to wonder
Say if you had another name
Would the person you know
Yes yourself,
Would you be the same?

One less minute
Or one more
The opening or closing
Of even one door

Different options
A different life
That minute, that name
May mean happiness or strife

To control the uncontrollable
Something we try to do
Don't lead yourself a stray
Be happy because you're you

THE SURREAL DEAL

You make my heart
Exude what eludes
So many
You lend everything splendid
To an understanding
That to most is surreal
I thank you for
Your gentle truths
And comforting smiles
I thank you
For facilitating a union
That feels no bounds
My heart pounds faster now

DRIVING GLOVES

The possibilities are endless of where we want to be
So much going on all at once so much we'll never see
We're living in the moment, now that moment's gone
If you feel stagnant remember, tomorrows another dawn

Get out and live, persevere,
Each and every day
But be careful not to over stretch
Or your soul will surely fray

Subconscious inner hysteria
About the want of all
It's good to keep your options open
But then it's that much easier to stall

What I mean by this you see
Is that you must choose to decide
Sometimes when all the doors are open
You're just cruising along for the ride

Get behind the wheel
Accomplish what you can
Life is certainly happening
It's time to take a stand

Put your foot down, take control
What is now will never be again
There are always other options, angles, and what ifs
We need more refrain to sustain with less disdain

TO BE YONDER

Dissolving attention
Dissention released
Awakening in a sleep
Intervention of a peace
Of mind, in a time
Not measured in line
With what's learned
In turn offering
Up moments in space
Reaching that eternal place
Footprints of fourth dimensions
That are forever free
Of definitive understanding
What is peculiar
About re-forming
With sensations
Of everything beyond ones self?

WHAT WAS THAT

What do you forget about
When remembering me
What about remembering
Will set you free
What do you need to remember?
Is it easier to forget?
How do we surrender
To the synchronicity
Don't have regrets
In letting go
Of what is no longer,
Including yourself

WHAT WAS THIS

What do you forget about
When remembering me
Trying harder is defeating
And I know you hate being
Defeated, you're so depleted
Eat it up, my advice to you
What about remembering
Will set you free
What do you need
To remember to remember?
It's easier I see in you
To just forget about it
How could you possibly surrender
To the proving ground
That wouldn't be sound

BARE BACKER

My illusions of grandeur
Take from my presence
Unwrapped, passed on
No surprises
About what is gone.
Why am I trapped?
In my miss?
Instinctually wanting bliss
Looking onwards
Looking backwards
Looking for words
That have been voiced
And heart felt
But through choice
Perhaps never dealt
With action.
Beyond the spoken
What is heard?
An insight into character?
What's more absurd?
Than the shirt that's gestured
From right off ones back
Would be this not the best cure?
When your tan's not quite black
Ponder forever in a second
Mind your delusions
For grandeur may be rejected
And verbal intrusions
That are deceptive inclusions
Of true nature at large
Who's in charge
Of affectation of credibility
It's time who takes control
Don't roll your eyes at me
Close them, what do you sense
Can you feel the world

Cont.

You have selected?
It's time to perfect it
Listen, hey you, a shirt I just found
I wonder who's affected
Was it passed on without thought?
Be precise, you are caught
With what you'll speak
Venting what's haught
May make trust weak
It only takes common sense
Yet not so common after all
A penny for your thoughts
Who would you help?
If they did fall
There's nobility
In the shirt you wear
If you would really pass it on
Here's mine if you're cold
And a bottle of Hawaiian tropic
If you get bold
Open yourself up
It's awareness we need
It's a lasting contribution
Strive to never mislead
Mean what you say
Forever is a long time
Through a redundant echo
Of semantic fallacies
It's not like it's worn out
From always giving it away
It's not even worn in
You're not wearing a shirt again today
It's hard to give the shirt off your back
When you don't even have one on
Oh and one more thing ;
Tearing the sleeves off to wipe clean
Your shit talk doesn't count.
Moving on…….

AUTOMATIC TELLER

Character is formed
It's built and warmed
With right and wrong
We're sometimes scorned
And perhaps we see
What we already know
From before we're conceived
What we're expected to show,
What we learn to believe
Is based on specifics
So prolific and exact
We deceive the terrific
We always need to have tact,
Are you suited to the conformity
Of this time and place
The uniformity....for most
Allows an untrue brace.
Is being accepted with worth
Really understood
Why does the sense become counterfeit
Do we forget that our birth
Is already perfection
Opportunity on this earth
Becomes limited
Because of the many
That foot print the bill
But are so petty
Never getting their fill
All has to be revised
You can't buy account ability
We all need to realize
We're governed by senility
For reasons in our face
Most of which are not admitted
To consumed in this rat race
Only a rat can win, what a disgrace

Cont.

We need to SPEARHEAD positive change
And rearrange electing folk who should be rather committed
Please withdrawal from the conditioning
And bank on the goodness in your character
Don't think everybody will branch off
Simplicities somehow become tarnished by status
It's to bad really if you never cheque regret
Payment is due
Don't withdrawal from humanity
We're all equally indebted in the end
Invest all in nurturing
Finance forever with love
Richness should have little to do with money
So may SINNERS concerned so much with the wrong currency
Deposit you insatiability in a locked in term
This should all be of the ultimate interest
Don't be afraid to make change
Spend your time with a conscious I plead
Indeed I'll lend this to you

POINT TAKEN

Muti layered dimensions
Of intellectual intentions
A complexity of emotion
Lends feeling
To devotion.
The information
You receive
Sometimes may deceive
Why believe this?
Isn't it all the same?
The interpretation game
Can be one
But never won

HEY NORM

If Ordinary is
Potentially scary
Is extra ordinary
Really very daring
What are you
Caring about
As these day
Play out on
Their brief stay
Hardly individually briefed
As the mighty
Hale supreme
Muting the truth
What points of view
Do you claim on que
I'm claiming askew
Is what you do
What ought you to?
Pre conceived actions
Deliver certain satisfactions
What's to believe
When what's up your sleeve
Is revealed
Why conceal prospective
It's not audacious
To care through
Everything
Make this the norm

SPECTRUMS

Light transcending
Bending as it lends
To dark
Too dark
It can be
As the continuum
Manifests
Redirects
And dissects
Our intellect
While adjusting
Our vision
Can we include what
Has eluded
Even the night
Can shine
With sprinkled hope
Piercing the armor
Of any inflicted darkness

FUSE SHAWN

Feeling closer to the dark
Than I am to the night
Feeling so far away from us
My sights are now locked
Meet me at midnight
In that special place
Right between asleep and awake
Guide me to divinity
I need to feel your kindred light
Warm my soul,
With your endless glow
Slowly as not to wake

SOUNDS LIKE NOW

The prison I sometimes find
In my mind
Is also a playground
And to stay sound
In the endless
You must befriend this
Imagine imagining
In the imagination
Of positive possibility
DO YOU HEAR THAT?
The sounds
Of staying
In the moment
Echoing as you read?
The recognition
Of repetition
That your thoughts
Think
Will lead
To an unveiling
Of perfection
That corresponds
With the absolute
These scribbles
Of understanding
Help to gather
Rather poignant
Individual specifics
That are prolific
In allowing
What needs to be felt?
And said
As well as
Written and read
So easy to unwrap
Your head around

BLURTATION STATION

Words are permanent
Any negative lent
To an un thought voice
Without choice
Can't be removed
Only abused
A faulty line
Shakes your foundation
Of what was once fine
Communication
Breakdown
An ominous frown
Becoming Numb
To the intentions
Behind verbal patchwork

METAMORPHING

A transmutation
Results in a celebration
Of the shedding of skin
At which time
The source on course
For showing your glowing
Emanating light
Is revealed
No longer concealed
By any flames of conflict
That preceded letting go
Now while you grow
It is possible to sublet
All you know
Through simply being

HOOK LINE SINKER

When propelling our visions
We can sway from our missions
For what we have caught
Along the way
As apposed per say
To what we've been taught
I thought
This today
And don't care to
Keep it at bay
It's not really the same thing
After it's steeped
Or is it?

DEPTHFLECTED PERCEPTION

Fire Flies dancing
Romancing, Illusions,
Conclusions of mystic
On the seek
Tend to be always
Ever so bleak, so to speak
Of an understanding
Thought necessary
The mind's demanding
Of sense can be very contrary
To what is actually real
Don't steal the magic of what you feel
With cognitive insecurity
What do your feelings see
When they are free
Of what is learned?
From time to time
You can sense the glow
I ask, please nurture this
While helping it to grow
I know you want to

REFLECTING SANCTITUDE

The sky is dropping
Letting in the stalking
Of this knight
Shining in the armor
Of its darkness
Senses protected
Special awareness
Projected
The heavens reflected
In the cosmos
Of the mind
I find sanctitude
With what eludes
The moods
Of our selection

TEEDER TODDERED

When dopamine is triggered
Does your depth get bigger
While your perception
Has spawned, what is beyond
That which is reasoned
With any personal treason
How can we equate justification
Into this equation
Of what temporarily pleases
You into that guaranteed state
That Is this.... surreal
Blending and bending
Into the fibers of your creature
Creating another feature
Staring at fluxes and fusions
Are you ever really happy
To be loosing
Your counter balance

ADAMS APPLES

As the pace becomes
More recognizably choice
The race wears on
Realizing your voice
Is equivalent to what rejoice
You feel when really listening.
This marathon equated
To the debate we call life
Is in its finality, decisive
Giving my newly sharpened teeth
A truly delicious meal
What appeal I find,
Myself digging in
Feeling at the same time
Letting go of the rind
To which you need not know
For nourishment.
A compelling strategy
For accomplishing
The exact pace
That is needed
While showing grace
In what is succeeded
I know of more
That is tougher to swallow
Than the core of it all

SECOND WIND

The notion of a breeze
Helps realize solace
In everything gentle
The calm preconceives
The whip cracking back
While the depths attack
What was not thought through
Concerned oh captain,
My captain is you.
Will you ride on this storm?
Is this all you've got
What have you fought for
Life is so manipulated
Now you are re-born
Into this destiny
Of an old explorer
To the earliest of times
Your mind re-forms
And the control of all
Is incalculably quickly
Frighteningly reduced
Oh it's just the beginning
The ocean has let loose
With no control the seas are spinning
You ride the wave of fate
Everything previous crashes
Like the wave goodbye
To which you bow
Fear, emotion, strength, devotion
Faults, curses, wrong doings, this ocean,
Verses repeating themselves,
With clasped hands
And salted lips
No longer a man
In your excuse for a ship
Reduced and used
This wasn't in the plans

Cont.

Feeling abused
It's now hard to take a stand
The powers that be
May be oblivious
To your deciding hour
Yet even with no power
You think not
While knowing anything
Beyond the unknown
Is finally impossible
This is clearly shown
With a magnitude
That has forever
Eluded conception
Setting out with no doubt
On your 4 hour tour
Had so much allure
I hope Marianne and Ginger
Were given permission to board
Weary skipper

R.J.D.

Heavy scented memories
Awakening time
In a thick cloud
Of scented rhododendron flowers
Marching through
In drawn out strides
Though tip towing with pride
As waves tickle the shore
In scores of gentle arrival
A wedding party
Clapping for more
While the sun kisses
Eternal wishes
Radiating, penetrating
The face of love
This now overgrown chapel
Is for a moment re-born
In the residues
Of a sensation
That exudes elation
From the past.
As the flowers smell lasts
Just long enough

This poem stemmed from a recollection of a chapel that my
grandfather, Dr. Robert John Donald Morris, had on his lakefront
property in Nelson BC in the late 70's. The property had been
in my family for over a hundred years before being recently sold.
My grandpa has come to pass but was once the head of the united
church of Canada and in the summer time with my grandma as the
consummate caretaker of all, he married a lot of lucky folk in this
dreamlike setting. I was quite young then but had recently been taken
back by a memory that stemmed from the wafting smell of a roddie
bush that lingered in the breeze on a summers walk in the Kootenays.

RUSTY COAT

Minding the flicker of your brain
As it is called upon to be quicker again
With refrain held at bay
In this day and age of what relevance
The aptitude dance is challenged
By the nano second
Forever unknowingly guessing
About the un flexibility of what's next
As the remoteness of control
Abruptly changes, rearranging matters
To yet another channel
I thought I heard this in the roosters crow
Get up, get up, get up
It's time to go again

A BEAUTIFUL FALL

Random patterns
Shattering all points of view
In between, what is the scene
North, East, South, West
Every time the best
On cue representation
There is no misconstrued
Presentation or intention
No intervention
When leaves fall
The call of what is wild
To witness has compiled
Ultimate timeless evidence
Of everything being
The same freelings
Not refraining of course
From its course of nothingness
That in this we want to reminisce
And sometimes dwell
Seeking to find randomness
In what shows purpose
For how the leaves fell

FINE PRINT

When moments turn
We learn, into memories
That free your soul
With reflections of time
That you find
In a ripple affect
Effectively you're absorbed
Into the surface tension
Of another
It's like no other
Purpose will do
So if two, become one
With intentions
Adding up to the sum
Of forever
This endeavor
Hand in hand
From a sometimes
Stand offish perspective
Is perhaps selected
From the master
Plan which if you read
The finer of print
Is to preserve individuality
While lending mortality
To the concept of being better
Perhaps than yourself
Thank you
    For the ongoing insight

ARE WE THERE YET

An American Dream
Dreamed not
While asleep
A Boler trailer
Setting free the streamline
Of an open road spree
With closed quarters
The tempered miles
Are getting shorter
Pressing rubber
Into the night
Public washrooms
Family fights
No end in sight
While hours pass
Waiting for a passing lane
Conversations and inclinations
About where to gas
Stomachs churn
Destinations tear by
Like perforations
In the journeys journal
What fuels the mystery
That unfolds at the end
Of this once respected road
Intersections dissecting
Beginnings with endings
That are thinning the tires
Still spinning through time
Looking for an off ramp
Pondering a u turn
Wondering whose turn
It is to drive you crazy
Straight ahead keeps coming
The trip rolls, the trailer holds
The weary course heads
Into the future

Cont.
What does suit you more?
Than coming full circle?
While the final resting spot
Is still an unknown?
For certain...
The children cry,
Are we there yet?!

OTHER THAN EVERYTHING

The allure of predictability
Residing in ordinary stability
A normal life
Is sequestered
Muting possibilities
Of gestured excitement
That may exist
Around every corner
Is this a gift
To realize the potential
Of the next hour
Or an insatiable attraction
When only a fraction
Of quality
May seep through
In the passing
Of in between
What you see
And what you do
Growing up
What does it take
To ween
The predictable
Unpredictability
Of the rush
That is life
What is sought
After we've fought
Our wars to the death
Why pretend to care
If our actions
Continuously fail
Continuously fall
We ignore and stall
On everything other
Than definitive normality
What morality
Will you choose?

MORNING MORPHING

A chalky feel
Steals the moment
As the melatonin pill
Slowly releases dissolve
Revolving the door
Of chemical relief
Lodged in my larynx
This time capsule
Is sluggish
In it's downgrade
Of my still conscious state
Leaving some debate
About the immediate
Restlessness of the moment
Measuring up your surroundings
The resilience of the crickets
Their squeaky wings speak
The echoing resonance
Of a stray dogs bark
Carries itself away
On the pliability
Of the fading day
Staring up in unrest
The questionable wobble
Of a poorly hung fan
Creates situational turbulence
That transcends the worry
Of a loose bolt spinning free
The musty breeze wafts
As the fan morphs
Into a flower
It's pedals blowing
In the counterfeit breeze
A computer on the headboard
Dims and brightens
Dissolving what heightens
Laying dormant

Cont.
Still, computing
It's cadence so suiting
A metro gnome
Dances for you
In the spectrums
Of illusion and thought
An intrusion is sought
By the consciousness beyond
The fan slices through the air
Into a ripple of dimensions
That if you stare
Long enough at
You may find
You awake to yourself
In time to hear the rain
Dampen the acute
Merger of all this

FULL CURL

An Aries man
Constantly sequestering
The life of a ram
The gesture is desired
To consult
The constellations
About the destination
Beyond
What is claimed
Known
How far is the stone
Thrown
Before
It skips past
Itself

GREETINGS

Reactive negativity
Influenced perhaps
By a distorted perception
A deflection of the now
Causing infection
Of and in itself
Collectively what's left to be
Is the unconsciousness
That can actually be seen
In almost every situation
An egoic salutation
While any conscious frustration
Manifests more
What's in store
May we ask
What's my task
There in lies
In their lies
The ultimate problem

PRICE CHECK PLEASE

A recycled breath
Prolonging existence
A tired rock
Beside a giant oak
A geeses flock
Swims by a lili pad afloat
Taking their shape
Reducing, fusing
Gaining and losing
Somehow altogether
Individually choosing
The same destination
Re-establishing themselves
Into each other
Everything alive
Pulsing dimensions
How long can we jive
In this galactic invention
What sanctity can survive
Let alone thrive
Without no more than good intentions
When everything that continues
To overwhelm on arrival
Is becoming short lived
How long till our drive will
Be overshadowed
By our self induction
To our decided power
Deciding which hour
Will be the last
That is known
Have we thrown
The towel over our senses
And immensity of Senselessness
Towards immediate utopia
In essence we are present

Cont.
In these precarious times
But our fleeting micro cosms
Are of macro proportions
Creating more distortions
In this frequency
Of Ill Logic

A WORLDLY MATTER

The calming softness
Of the cool air
Soothing in a delicious way
After the earth
Having kept at bay
The rains that saturate
This fruitful day
Joyous and animated
Enthusiastic and elated
To often we over estimate
Life, is thirsty now bursting
With a never duplicated
Existence, that our persistence
Is draining
Feel rejuvenation
In an attitude
That represents
Careful grace
For this space
Needs constant nurture
Support and create
A needed elation
In all that is
This life

SPLISH SPLASH

The intermittence of love
Like wipers washing away
The storms that be
Driving on, you encounter
That hazy uncertain spot
Between dusk and beyond
The tears form puddles
That pool and are muddled
Falling for the unknowing fool
Who like the wipers
In the cold wind of the now night
Thinks it is his only duty
To help keep your attention
On seeing clearly
Even though you know
Perfectly well
Amidst the spell
Of the beading rain
That your vision
It's perfectly fine

SKIN DEEP

A rascally way
For the most part
Of your adventurous days
Never in formation
The elation you felt
From being free
Was your decree....absolute
Now looking back
You're more easily able
To look further ahead
With the skin
You have now shed
Some have even said
You are more full,
Fully formed
Newly informed
About old habits
That constantly swarmed
It should be warned
That we did begin
With the 3 fated
Originated layers

ABSORBED

Falling colors,
Fall hollers
Leaves, leaving
Re-grounding
The sound brings
A following
Of movement
Only felt
The wind is stealth
And what's dealt
Lets us go
And for that moment
Time slows
As we remember
What we can't know
But yet are.
This rebirth
Of the continuum
Cyclically re-integrates
Itself with all
This happening
Is us, beyond feeling
Absorb the complete
Not feel defeat
In what isn't fair

CURVE BALLER

Natures hospital
Was once thought inexhaustible
This suspended sustainability
Is slowly subdued
While siphoning constitution
Out of this self induced illusion
Life is what…....
Is it that we are choosing
Slowly we are loosing
Our sensible ways
Laying dormant
With continuity gone
The morrow is spawned
The marrow of dawn
Is leaking sleekly
Into a bleak unfolding.
What lies at our feet
In disguise, we disgust
Oh our lust
For luxury
Has us throwing
Curve balls to the wind
With blown humanitarian values
Landing by the ways side
Which side will you take?
Who dares to stand tall,
And derive pride
In how we may survive
What do we source
As the inevitable course
A colliding force
Is beckoning our call
And as we stall
Basking in the chosen
Purpose ignorance
We ignore what

Cont.

Is in store
This erratic devolution
May have many a solution
But just awareness
In all fairness
Seems like an excuse
To segregate into classes
That see so many thinking
They're above the masses
And unless we all choose
Equality with a conscious,
And how could you
Not want this,
Then our luxuries
Will be no more
What do we really need?
Is what we really need to do
PROGRESSIVE ACTION
Satisfaction must not elude
Compassion for all
The faction of longevity
Is simply now
To live simply
And give back
To our true nature

DRAMA SCHOOLED

Hello friend
I said to the eternal moment
Choosing to lay rest
As best I could
To human drama
Now where, I am here
While I search to hear solace
Accepting what is
As a humble impromptu understanding
Through this choice
That these words
I voice to all
Become the call
Of contentment
And so it is
Said the timely companion.
I pondered,
So this is that so

If Your over exposed
Will you under react
To compensate for the fear
Of not keeping things in tact

LONG FADE

Residuality
Residual duality
Re-inventing
To who's reality
Are we consenting?
Intervene
An intervention
Why is it so hard
To get your own attention
Shattering light bulbs
Before they go off
With no filament
You get your fill of mental
Cognitive intuition
Bringing strength
To fruition
Learning to live
With how you feel.
What used to be
A dull glow
Was disguised
By sparks
Once illuminating
A loud bark
That has now faded
Quietly
Into the dark
I energize my light
Without spite
To what
Has been
All Squared Up

SQUARE OFF

You're drowning me
While swimming free
In my mind I find
You not to care
All is fare
So they say
As I continue to pray
For more love
Than war
As these circles
Your spinning
Still swimming
Are the beginning
Of the end
Holding my breath
Turning blue,
Right on queue
I am able to view
A time lapse
Of your laps
Ending in collapse
Of this lap dog.
With no more restraint
It seems quaintly so
That my leash snaps
Straight lining
This time
Freedom is mine.
Now and again though
I still tend
To the question:
Why the circles…
When you are
Such a square.

THINK ABOUT IT

An evaluation of thought
Out to reveal
How experience is affected
And how it is one does deal
With circumstances and chances
And what is actually real
Romancing what stances
You take, how do you feel
What do you give
How do you live
Energy emitted
The synergy re-fitted
Attracting like minds
With positivity I find
That I find positivity
And visa versa
Not a master
Card curser
What's given?
Is received
Appraising out put
Helps to believe
In the power
Of thought

SLUMBER PARTY

Sleep as a drug could be the most addictive I know
But because we need it to live and to grow
Do we really relate to the escape it can provide
From the hardships in life we sometimes want to hide

I crave the subconscious to be lost in my dreams
Because here nothings ever as real as it seems
This delusion wouldn't seem as dangerous as some
Yet the strange comfort it provides is hard to overcome

No motivation to experience, the days they roll by
Yet R.E.M. for some reason is a strange depressing high
Though not one in which most would care to hang on
Like a child your eyes shut, and everything is gone

But unlike a child, you should know that this is not the case
Yet what you know seems not to matter, and time you continue to
       waste
It's all a contradiction though in who I want to be
But before I can be anything shouldn't I be me?

Sure this seems cut and dry when you've got you figured out
But it's not as simple for that someone, filled with confusion and
       doubt
And everybody is at times, but in ourselves we must still believe
Don't try to escape….. what is real,
                                      Are we that naïve?

TARGET PRACTICE

We are living and pondering
Existing tragedy
Reasoning with what
Becomes unreasonable
Money blind sex ample
While we trample
Revise before demise
When action is muted
While promises scream on
We become our own obstacles
Absorbed in tomorrows dawn
Insatiable at best
So what…, is equality
Ever really shown
Nothing's equally grown
We don't need a ruler
To erase the lines
En guard
We're over drawn
Drop your weapons
Of mass destruction

BEAN THERE

Diesel clouds back lit
Lofting thick, on every corner
The crowds unaffected
As the early morning sun
Arrives everyone a new day
In the highest capital
City in the world.
La Paz Is fast to awake
And I take it that some
Have yet to sleep
The golden light creeps
Up cobblestone streets
As the nights last fight
Disappears up the storied walls
In the narrowest of alleys
Reflecting a time
No longer still
Reminiscent in the glisten
I listen to the hustle bustle
The scenes however acute
Are bombarded by the infinite
Frames per second
This movie is unfolding
Beholding all the more
Than four dimensions
In every direction, the selection
Of decisions is drowned down
By the white bright noise
Of gentle chaos, as each player
Is again tossed into their positions
Taking part in fulfilling
The happenings of this day
A foray of café's
Comes into view
Alas absorbing you
A Bob Marley tune
Graces the senses

Cont.
Of more than the ear
And we decide here
Is a good place to reflect
While quenching and getting stimulated
On a quaint bench seat
Of a nostalgia filled diner
That contained within its walls
So many of the finer
Artifacts of this vast past
Still not as fast
To be replaced or discarded
In a society I regard as
Functioning perhaps in a less
Far fetched way, even though
Staying by necessity, less advanced
Based on semantics not as frantic
To consume beyond their means.
Oh the smell of freshness
Coming from the roasting coffee beans
Has so much allure
Over the instant café cure
That is traditionally stirred
Into the mornings vaso
The bistro held its own
As a time capsule, at least to me
The Western free bird.
Some still so falsely content
Waiting in their cages
To be fed the daily bread
Of our societal disorder
I hold back on my regular order
Of replenishing coco tea
The so called free world
Hurls to the illegal way side
While continuing to hide the truth
My eyes let loose
On what was being displayed

Cont.

Yet fitting right in, an array
Of gramophones in the shape of flowers
Old corroded pieces of time
No need of any longer showing the hour
The powerful surroundings captivated
Elevating an awareness of simplicity
With intricacy that was soothing to me
Transistor radios, telescopes
A plethora of typewriters, old doctors totes
Revolvers hung from the wallpapered walls
And the call of the wild hung tall
With clay bullets and rust flaked barrels
Positioned I wonder purposely
Above maps that now longer harrowed
Any resemblance of the countries
We know in our "modern day"
There were tinctures in cabinets
Embalming healing recipes from the past
Surveying equipment & a push button register,
That was still performing its task.
As we paid our bill
I stood still getting my last fill
Of wonderment while noticing
For the first time
The entire establishment
Was as full as full could be
I then realized between
The step back into real time
And my company
I had been so completely there
It was as if we had been just two
What an exuberating feeling!
So with this and so much care for you
I remember opening the door
For my beautiful miss to walk through
Seeing there were folk waiting
I paused to give you a kiss

Cont.

Pondering all time
That we were obviously in
We both felt the afternoon begin
Walking off hand in hand
Aimlessly into the hustle bustle
Creating our own history in the mystery
With the unfolding trivia in wonderful Bolivia
Singing to the tune of satisfied souls

MEGGA WHAT?

Living on the edge
Of a clouded lightning bolt
Blinded and burning
It's more than a jolt
Then the lights go out
Rushing in come thunder shakes
Now you sanity is rattled
Your desire is now to awake
Yet it isn't a dream
But without any doubt
You've hidden yourself away
And now you want to get out
But you are already here
Where you always reside
Everything's so crystal unclear
From yourself did you hide
Then with one flash of light
That rips through you at warp speed
You get some high voltage insight
And with simple choice you are freed

MUD BOGGIN

My ability to effectively change; to re-arrange
Was hindered by my mind........strange
Because in there I was fine
And in time I hit the gas
Back up to speed is what I needed
Going fast yet in reverse
Same destination what a curse
Never learned, for what I yearned
Was an action, satisfaction
Another blown tire
Now no traction
Can't find the inner state
It's fate that's left
Turn straight I guess
That's right, a mess
Set up for disappointment
I again confess
But with choices and control
We are blessed
I'll have you know
It's ok to communicate
With your internal voice
It helps elevate
Your traction
Even if you have
Your slicks on
In a mud bogg

WELCOME SPIRIT WOLF

A wolf enters the room
Once he stood
As the wolf would stand
But there was no room,
Or maybe there was more
More for the wolf
The room is now mine
Mine for this time being
The spirit of the wolf
I fail to understand
Curious, Puzzled, Angry, Frightened
Am I as I awake
As is the wolf as it stares
The eyes so mysterious and powerful
Enlightening all
My own overflowing with fear
Breathless, unsure
Panting, so pure
Overpowered by its presence
Perched on the floor
Snarling a vicious snarl
I am suddenly the intruder
My heart races on
Chasing dawn
As I seem to awake again
Still staring
What am I sharing
Now more awake
I am my subconscious
Conscious I now see
So vividly the wolf
Where's the wolf
My heart slows down
My snubbed....conscious catches up
My mind is now crisp
So very aware

Cont.
Heightened, still scared
An unintentional dare
To the wolf...........
A chill still present
The spirit still looms
The unexplained, the unknown
The wolf will again be free
To howl and roam

LEARNING CURVE

Relinquishing desire
To have explanations
Distinguishing the fire
Of any perpetrations
That may or may not
Not make sense
It easier perhaps
When not on the fence
About experiences
That may be generously
Lent to you
Inducing truths
Empirically bound
By dimensions
Only found
In the journey
Not sound
For learned reality

DESTITUTION... SOLUTION?

Outcasts of society
Fear of the possibility
Fact; this could be you or me
Was it once an attempt to be free

To escape from conditions
You don't fit in
Too accept less and be fulfilled
This is certainly not a sin

I see the homeless, some are begging,
Dumpsters filtered through
This makes me feel a longing sadness,
By choice or necessity is this true

Are these pre-conceived roles
Like puppets on their ropes
This at times is the majority
Although I do still see some hope

There are reasons people live this way
A sequence of events led to the day
What skills through time are held at bay
How much of society thinks it's simply Ok?

ELEPHANT SHOES

I asked with a smile
Just for a while
Would you please
Could you please
Forget the words
To the story of this world
And remember our eternity
In such a captivating bliss
Your gentleness sooths
And if you are also moved
Then please don't miss me
In anything forever
Kiss me at last
It's the most clever way
To tell me everything....
I LOVE YOU

DETAILS DETAILS

You are by all means
The catalyst for me being lifted
So gifted are you.
In our union lies a truth
That has taken flight
Soaring into a luminous light
Above the eternal
I see all disappear
Reappearing as the dizzying perspective
Allows a selective understanding
Of only the most important details

ATTENTION PLEASE

A riot in ones mind
That obscurely caters to thoughts combined
With ones you remember, ones you know
And thoughts that are somehow before processed let go
Diverse and vibrant, drab and dark
Every single thought engrains a mark
In your psyche, and imprint of you
Or simply imprinted, do they give you a clue
To the vast possibilities of who we are
And actually where it is we reside among the stars
Shinning so brightly giving life like the sun
And know I don't mean the Hollywood stars,
Adding to life's conundrum
So many thoughts, from the small and fleeting
To the large, powerful, and often misleading
Ones you dismiss and ones you miss
And ones perhaps making you smirk from reading this
Each and every thought has a role to play
Either way….. I recon they should coincide, not hide
From/with the choices that effect how we live each day

DEVILUTION

What not long ago was a plethora of power and force
Natural predators roaming free
Is now over taken by our human collision course
With all of our shrapnel and high speed debris

It certainly wasn't that long ago
That our mortal selves peered out from caves
The eco system was balanced within itself
Now most of those habitats seem to be paved

From the depths of the oceans
To the highest snow covered peaks
In every single direction and more
The human race simply reeks

Such a monstrous havoc
On where it's all taking shape
Shrinking the natural worlds habitat
Cleaning balance right off the global plate

Can we remedy our compiling problems
That inevitably "our intellect" did create
We once wondered if we could co-exist
Now exactly the opposite is a grave debate

COOL IT

who are we
are we who
who we are
is alive today
7 degrees
before decimation
so many craving
separation
more water
is starting to boil
with the worlds turmoil
purify me

MINDING MANNERS

I am more concerned
About remembering to say please
Than I am about loosing my keys
Our manners with tact
And how one does act
Is reflected
With your q's
And your p's
It's so important
Habitually engrain
Be polite and always refrain
From lashing out
Verbal bashing
No doubt
Is a mark
On more than your name
Send your message
With kind intent
And represent
The delivery, man
A lock can always be picked

WINDSHIELD WIPERS

Your mind hits rush hour
All your thoughts searching to get somewhere
It all adds up to a standstill
You are swarmed,
By the potential of everything
Attacking at will,
Will you allow defeat
Justified history
It seems to repeat
Conditioned to live, and this I see
Is a product of a scared society
Not able to make a sacrifice
Too risky when you don't hold the dice
Will you ever know until you do
The traffic subsides
Your thoughts roll on
Is clarity possible?

Courage can go beyond the realm of analysis and logic. Knowing risks and calculating involvement in endeavors, is different than being thrown into a situation, or presented with one (as another way of putting it), and reacting to the necessity of the moment. In certain happenings if you allowed yourself time to process the consequences and ramifications, actions would be, a lot of the time for most people, non-existent. So if you don't process the negative side, that doesn't mean you are somehow not aware of it. Yet courage allows * "no simple explanation for anything important" and yet a focus that can be so absolute it can be beyond comprehension as if super sub conscious. Without this precluding happening there would most likely be none. Therefore, courage itself in extreme cases may supersede and is outright essential to the actions we associate it with.

* "The human tragedy consists in the necessity of living with the consequences under pressure, under pressure."

* Quote from "The Tragically Hip" song Courage

NOT TO IGNORE

Imagine if ignorance did prevail
Suddenly no wind to fill your sail
From hindsight you're no longer able to learn
And just for one more chance do you yearn

If this sounds familiar than open your eyes
Before it's too late and you're filled with cries
That everyone hears and tries to subdue
You never thought it could happen to you

Prevention is key, can't we think enough ahead
How much will you learn after you're dead
Take the time now to practice what you know
Be strong enough not to let yourself go

We disregard what's proven to be true
And with a dash of time the hazards just stew
Until the pot reaches a violent boil
And over it blows creating turmoil

Of course it's nothing you expected or wanted to relate
While the sad thing is, it's by choice not by fate
Now you're faced with what you already knew
You're a fool you let ignorance happen to you

STOKER POKER

Once you're up
You tend to feel fine
Try to utilize this life
Instead of wasting time

Motivate yourself
Get up with the rising sun
Once you're up and see this beauty
Sleeping becomes less fun

It's easy to roll over
Ten more minutes is all you want
Soon ten turns into a hundred
And the wasted hours come back to haunt

In between sleep and awake
A fantastic state fore sure
Everybody loves it
But dozeing's just a blur

It seems that if you sleep to much
It will take its toll
Always groggy and yawning
It's no fun believe me I know

So get up and live
Take advantage of the time you've got
Inspire yourself to take life on
Not lay in bed and rot

SAULEMN

When something is missing
And can't be returned
We must try to accept
That whatever we have learned

Because of this something
Is better than not
Even though a part of me is gone
An understanding is sought

But it will never make sense
Until in a place when it can
Don't try and figure it out
It's not your master plan

But a plan all the same
That in you're blessed to partake
Enduring all pain and pleasures
Some things end up a mistake

So if you are feeling down
When the hard times start to crawl
These especially are the times
That we must always recall

The something that is missing
Isn't gone or missing at all
We must look a little deeper
I sure do miss you my friend Saul

LETS RUMBLE

A familiar tension hangs
On the effervescent
Yet unusually still air
An intervention between
The sounds that cannot be seen
Bangs and with that I stare
Into the mosaic of this afternoon
Waiting for a besieging jolt
Of a thunderous bellow......
Precluding this was a moody
Interlude reflected in the hectic
Yet perfect unruliness
That the ways of the day
Poured down on me
Nourishing and flourishing
With an aggressive brilliance
Sustenance here prevails
As the sail of life
Is thrust by the wind
Full and robust
On it's own mission
Like rootlets I notice
Exercising there smiles
Suiting their needs
To balance and breathe
Stretching upwards
Through a freshly laid
Newly paved
Suffocating grave
For the underlying aliveness
Still obsessing with life
By being unknowingly spry
A car drives by
On this stretch of road
That has laid no hold
On the nature below
As mother earth yawns

Cont.
Another disenchanted yawn
The spawn of the 1ˢᵗ thunderbolt
Is thrown from the ground
Making a sounds that parallels
The embedment of all
Dynamic brilliance
Bestowing a needed connection
Of everything with everything
As my ears continued to ring
I heard the sound of a horn
Realizing in the downpour's encore
Someone had stopped to pick up
This saturated wanderlusterer

BELONGINGS

We are so distracted
By all attachments
We perceive
And believe
Our identities naively
Are apart of our belongings
Inanimate fantasia
Will deaden
What amazes ya
Within the simplicities
Of the universitality
In aliveness

RENOVATION INNIHILATION

Forever missed, never returned
Agro pissed, my belongings were burned
It happened so quickly, away for one night
When I got home, the fire burned bright
Suddenly ending; unforeseen change
The lack of respect is slightly deranged
A part of me is gone, although I am still me
The treasures I've lost, are now eternally free
We hoard things away, little bits of the soul
Not expecting their absence, the loss takes its toll
Realizing the past is not where I am at
Doesn't take away from the sorrow
And won't get my treasures back
Missed communication combined with selfish motivation
Allowed another individual, to create temporary annihilation
Of saved possession carried through time
Torched and now ashes,
an inconceivable crime
- cock sucker

GOOD LUCK TO YOU

Because we are what we've lived
Do our memories rule all?
If you're not on the up
Then are your down from a fall

It seems one or the other
And never much in between
Indicative in part due to circumstance
My luck has been at either extreme

264

PRECISELY

An acute darkness
Towers above
The ancient immensity
Of the wise yellow cedars
The mute of a lark
Is deeper than the mark
Left by the meditative silence
That accompanies this perfection
The fathomless depth
Of this night
Is in harmony and free
Of anything to spite
The lark ruffles its feathers
And together
With the shimmering sky
Takes flawless flight
Balancing equilibrium
As the first leaves of fall
Randomly displace
Falling in to exact place
Amongst the precision
Of the unified forest

PRISMS

Rain rain nourishing the day
A cycle of necessity
Blessing all, with an array
Of glistening drops
Sounds that sooths,
Particles of infinity
And emotions that move
The sun it's not gone
Just resting its rays
On blankets of dreams
Helping prolong life's stay

A STEP BACK IN TIME

I just read some thoughts of nature
From some time ago
I found when I was reading them
That they allowed me to grow

A poem written by my great gran
About 70 years before
The connection I felt I wanted to endure
I couldn't help but want a little more

It talked about loving everything
For this was certainly her from birth
It talked about how lucky we are
To be on this beautiful wonderful earth

Take the time out to experience all beauty
To talk to the flowers the birds and the trees
Let them know that you love them
Open you heart in order to see

Stroll through an enchanting forest
Seek out misty groves and shady nooks
Absorb yourself in a mossy bank
Beside a gentle murmuring brook

Allow it to tell its secrets
Perhaps confide and tell some too
Visiting together with the notion of one
Become friends while passing through

What an intriguing destination it has
Telling of where it's going and where it's been
It tells of all the fabulous sounds it's listened to
And all the marvelous sights it's seen

Cont.

It has gazed at the glorious sunrise
Each dawn of every new days wake
It has watched the sky paint with golden rays
Gladdening all for heaven sake

It's journeyed through desolate mountains
Where the wild beasts have their lairs
It has heard chilling howls of the hungry wolf
And the fiercest growls of the bears

It glides through the cool green arches
Where the ferries make their homes
Here I find that I can sit for hours
Never really feeling alone

I do watch these fantastic dainty ferries
All floating on silver gauzy wings
Dancing so peacefully everywhere
Eternally happy and ever enchanting

Bubbling through decadent flowered meadows
Where animals feed on the luscious grass
It waves to the beauty beyond the bank
Promoting growth as it goes past

Oh it's a lovely cheerful brook
So ever wonderfully kind
It carves new paths to the future
Helping turn the wheels of time

It carries a burden of secrets
Its silence will closely keep
Till it glides through the dark intriguing gates
Where time and eternity meet

Cont.
As I pause awhile to listen
And gaze into the silent dark
I hear sweet music riding the wind
Like the sound of the angles harp

We still have the chance to experience
All of this beauty and awe
Inspire to be apart of the enchantment
We're blessed to see, not because you saw

Search for all of the rainbows
For love is the pot of gold
Allow yourself enlightenment
To yourself is the key that all hold

To do everything that there is to do
Isn't possible with our limited time
Or is it? What's everything?
A question that's on my mind

70 years ago life was more simple
Perhaps more time to appreciate and feel
If it's all relative, than answer me this
How do so many loose sight of what's real

Always be in touch with the ferries and the streams
The intoxication can fill your soul
It's not something that could ever be defined
Lending to moments that help us feel whole

While we're here search for all beauty,
Create goodness while it all unfolds
Try to calm your restless spirit
It is peace we need as an ultimate goal

It makes me silent to think of those
Who can't find the aforementioned until gone up above
Please do your best to embrace what is precious
And promote all life, filling it always with love

Y SOL PERFECTO

The sol casts its glow
And although intangible
We know its existence
Is responsible for what
We know to exist
Like our own shadow
Never mucho consado
To just be in contrast
We see the rays of light
And an un detachable
Untouchable sight
Of our permanent
Impermanence
It is only real
In relation to self and sun
Does it help to be one
Are you picking up
What the shadow's
Throwing down
Is it real, is it not
I oh forgot
Just one thing:
Beunas Seurte

SAULICE

The sun watches
Over all
And over all
So many sons watch
Balancing dark
With a balancing spark
The balancing of light
Takes away any slight
About vibrancies above
Infusing love
With the Saulitude
Of this life
Oh you are missed.

—